TOO MUCH GOVERNMENT!

GUIDEPOSTS TO CHANGE!

DANA L. TURK

PREAMBLE

We the People of the United States, in Order to form a more perfect Union, establish Justice, insure domestic tranquility, provide for the common defense, promote the general welfare, and secure the Blessings of Liberty to ourselves and our Posterity, do ordain and establish this

Constitution
For the
United States of America.

ACKNOWLEDGMENTS

Thanks to my family and friends who have encouraged me to pursue this work. Thanks to our Founding Fathers and Creators of the U.S. Constitution, and thanks to the First Amendment to that Constitution that gives me the freedom to write the messages herein without fear of persecution.

A special thanks to the U.S. Presidents, Congressional Leaders in both the House and Senate, and the State, County and City Governments for giving so much substance and validation to this book. If it weren't for the greed and corruption of our Governments, I would have had nothing to write about.

"It is important (likewise) that the habits of thinking in a free country should inspire caution in those entrusted with its administration, to confine themselves within their respective constitutional spheres; avoiding in the exercise of the powers of one department to encroach upon another. The spirit of encroachment tends to consolidate the powers of all the departments in one, and thus to create, whatever the form of government, a real despotism."
-
George Washington's, Farewell Address to the people of the United States, Sep. 17, 1796

CONTENTS

FORWARD

After the first publication of this book, I was accused of wanting to change everything but keeping my own benefits intact. That is not a true assumption. We need to change the parts of our government that require change. Yes, I am a Veteran, I served my country and went where my Government sent me at great cost to my family, just as everyone who has served has done -- some at a greater cost than others. I believe Veterans have earned and deserve the benefits they were promised by the Government they serve without fear of those benefits being changed, reduced or deleted because of budgetary restraints. Yes, I am retired and able to receive my social security. Like most of the people in this country I have worked and contributed to social security. Even the Military and Government Civil Service employees contribute to social security. This is not an entitlement it is a right. The right to be able to withdraw the money we have deposited throughout our working lives. The right to be able to support ourselves in our senior years at somewhat better than poverty levels. It is not just my benefits that are addressed in this book, it is the benefits of all the people in this country. It is about a Government which forgets who they work for.

I was also accused of regurgitating Fox News. I never claimed this book was anything new, in fact, I admitted in the beginning the only thing new here would be some of the solutions. Have you ever thought our Government was out of control? Have you ever wondered why it takes so many people to run and work for the various departments of Government? So, have I! I began looking for the answers to these questions. This book doesn't answer all your questions but sheds light on how government became the monster it is.

"Oh, what tangled web we weave, when first we practice to deceive" – 1808 Scottish Poet Sir Walter Scott

This quotation from Sir Walter Scott's poem sums up what our Government has been doing since 1789. A tangled web woven of lies, coercion, corruption and abuse of the Constitution, the American people and our rights. I have researched a considerable number of sources to acquire the information presented in this book including records from the National Archives, the Office of Personnel Management, the Congressional Record and the Library of Congress as well as news and internet sources. I have spent countless hours researching the issues that plague our lives because of actions taken by an out
of control Government. In my research, I have found contradiction, confusion and ambiguity in just about every bill passed by Congress in the last 225 years, but I have also found outrageous lies in some of the email and rumors about our Government. In this book, I will attempt to present the truth about our Government (the <u>Good</u>, the <u>Bad</u>, the <u>Ugly</u> and the <u>Indifferent)</u> and will present solutions to fix it.

If I have found anything in my research that even hinted there was a problem with the Government you will see it here; but, if I found anything that corrects a false rumor, it will be here as well. I am not going to pull any punches; therefore, I may upset or offend some or even a lot of people. If I offend you, I suggest you take a good look in the mirror, because if you are offended you may be part of the problem.

This book is about change, about reform and about stopping the abuse of the Constitution and our rights. It is also about trying to present some solutions to make things right. If ruffling some feathers and dispelling some rumors along the way helps to make things right, I hope you can accept that too.

I am not presenting anything new here, and I won't guarantee that some of this won't bore you to tears, but it all has a purpose. I am consolidating everything you may have felt or heard for years about the government into one place. I will try to keep the boring parts brief.

One of the greatest problems most writers and people in general have when writing or talking about the Government is that it's easy to point out government faults, but it's much more difficult to present reasonable and viable solutions. There are as many different solutions to the country's faults as there are people living here. Some are similar, some are vastly different, but all are good. We need a common solution which enables all of us to work together for the common good. One hundred people working on a problem with their individual solutions accomplishes nothing. One hundred people working together to achieve one goal accomplishes much. Imagine what three hundred million people can do. It's a teamwork thing. T.E.A.M. "Together Everyone Accomplishes More". We can no longer be the "I" generation. There is no "I" in "TEAM" and we must make taking control of the Government a TEAM effort.

I am going to present solutions to fix the problems as I see them. Whether you agree with my solution or not, it may provide enough inspiration that together we can come to a viable solution - a solution we can all agree on and will work together to get our government back on track.

There are no quick and easy fixes here. The Government, Big Bank and Big Industry have been entrenched and fortifying their positions for most of the last 100 years. Effecting change is going to take time, resources and energy, but most of all it's going to take *We, The People*, standing together and speaking up in a unanimous voice that we are going to have change, that we are taking control of the government back.

Robert Kennedy once said *"There are those who look at things the way they are, and ask Why... I dream of things that never were, and ask Why Not?"* To which his brother President John F. Kennedy added *"We need men who can dream of things that never were"*.

If you are ready to dream of things that never were, at least not in most of our lifetimes, then continue reading and let's ask <u>why not</u> and work together to build a better government and a better and stronger country.

The United States of America is a great country with a great system of government which was founded on the principle of a government OF, BY, and FOR the People. Unfortunately, today most of our elected officials are more of, by and for their own wealth, special interest groups, big banks and following the party line and have forgotten that they are hired by us, the people, act in our behalf.

To eliminate redundancy, Government throughout this book refers to all Governments, Federal, State, County, City and Township.

I am not a radical, nor am I a sheep. I served in the Military for almost 42 years combined active duty, reserve and retired reserve.

I believe in My God, My Country, My Government and My Family, but I believe that one of those four - like a child out of control - needs some guidance to bring it back on track. I can't do it alone. I need your help.

Hopefully, the pages that follow will help cut through the rhetoric, minutia and legalese to show that our Government is and has been out of control and needs the people to stand together to bring democracy back to the United States.

"My reading of history convinces me that most bad government results from too much government." - Thomas Jefferson

"Unless the States will content themselves with a full and well-chosen representation in Congress and vest that body with absolute powers in all matters relative to the great purposes of war, and of general concern ... we are attempting an impossibility, and very soon shall become (if it is not already the case) a many-headed monster--a heterogeneous mass--that never will or can steer to the same point." – George Washington

WHAT IS A BILLION?

A billion of anything is hard to imagine without some type of reference. Very few people have ever seen a billion dollars.

Here's what a Billion looks like:

One Billion Seconds ago, it was 1985

One Billion Minutes ago, it was 112 AD.

One Billion Hours ago, it was 114155 years ago, and our ancestors were cavemen.

One Billion Miles is 1984 round trips to the moon. (One round trip to the moon being 504,176 miles)

While these figures are fresh in you mind consider this: In 2007 after Hurricane Katrina destroyed much of New Orleans, a Senator from Louisiana asked Congress for $250 billion to help rebuild the city. In 2007, New Orleans had a population of about 485,000 people. If you do the math, 250 billion would mean that every Man, Woman and Child in the City of New Orleans would receive $515,811. A family of 4 would get approximately $2,063,244.

It's obvious that our Government has no clue as to how much a billion is and, based on the National Debt, spends approximately one billion dollars, that's $1,000,000,000 every seven hours. Twenty-Four Hours a day, seven days a week, three hundred sixty-five days a year, 24/7/365. Where did the Government get the power to recklessly over spend? I'm going to explain the answer in the chapters that follow.

"It is incumbent on every generation to pay its own debts as it goes. A principle which if acted on would save one-half the wars of the world." - Thomas Jefferson

"To contract new debts is not the way to pay old ones." – *George Washington*

THE CONSTITUTIONAL ABUSE

THE AMENDMENTS – These are the most controversial and abused amendments to the Constitution and those that need the most reform or repeal.

The Bill of Rights

The 2nd Amendment - Right to keep and bear arms.

The 10th Amendment - Reinforces the principle of Federalism by stating that the Federal Government possesses only those powers delegated to it by the States or the People through the Constitution.

Governmental Change Amendments

Amendments that change the way our Government functions and establishes State and Public controls.

The 12th Amendment - Revises Presidential Election Procedures. Revises the Electoral College.

The 16th Amendment - Permits Congress to Levy Income Taxes without sharing it with the States.

The 22nd Amendment - Limits the number of Terms of Office a President may serve.

The 27th Amendment - Delays laws affecting when a congressional pay raise may take effect.

General Change Amendments

These are General Amendments that provide for governing specific issues.

The 14th Amendment - Defines Citizenship, contains a privileges and immunities clause and a due process clause.

I've highlighted and referenced these Amendments because it is these Amendments where our Representatives have not voted in favor of the people they represent. In many of these they have voted in direct contrast to the benefit of the people and the Constitution. These Amendments and how they have been abused will be presented at length in the chapters which pertain to them.

These referenced Amendments and the Congressional duties and responsibilities (which are referenced in the last chapter) will become important as you will see.

"Truth will ultimately prevail where there are pains taken to bring it to light." – George Washington 1794.

WHO IS TO BLAME?

To resolve the issues facing the People of the United States as they concern our Government, we must first identify who is to blame for the problems. For the better part of the last 100 years the Republicans have blamed the Democrats and Democrats have blamed the Republicans for the woes of the country. It is interesting when taking a closer look at the Parties the Democratic representatives are predominately lawyers while the Republican representatives are predominantly businessmen. But the fact is, it is the parties who have created the problems we face today. The Parties, however, are just the catalyst and not the cause.

The unfortunate truth is, We, The People are to blame! We have given away our liberties and freedoms to politicians, power brokers, big business and bankers since this country was founded.

The 10th Amendment - Reinforces the principle of Federalism by stating that the Federal Government possesses only those powers delegated to it by the States or the People through the Constitution.

But who is running the Country? If you think for even a minute that "We, The People," have a voice in who is running this country, think again. We are the victims of one of the greatest hoaxes ever created. The hoax being the belief that "We, The People" matter to government.

Money has ruled this country since the days of Washington, Adams, Jefferson and Hamilton. England's taxation and theft of the riches of the colonies spurred our forefathers into action and brought about the Declaration of Independence. Our founding fathers were some of the wealthiest men in the revolutionary United States and had the most to lose to English taxation. Throughout the revolutionary war, they increased their wealth by supplying (selling) valued materials from their plantations to the continental Army and Navy and continued to supply those materials while in Office. Their wealth gain wasn't even close to or as blatant as what our politicians are hauling away today.

Thomas Jefferson warned in 1802:
"I believe that banking institutions are more dangerous to our liberties than standing armies. If the American people ever allow private banks to control the issue of their currency, first by inflation, then by deflation, the banks and corporations that will grow up around the banks will deprive the people of all property - until their children wake-up homeless on the continent their fathers conquered."

During this early period of our history only land owners and big industrialists could vote. It is also true the only people who could run for office were these same land owners and industrialists. The common man was left to follow and trust whoever the wealthy put into office. As the country grew, the wealth of the founding fathers and their heirs was surpassed by the wealth generated by those gaining riches from the westward movement. The Railroad, Steel, Coal, and precious metals like Gold and Silver, advanced families like the Carnegie's, Rockefeller's, Morgan's, and Guggenheims into the political spotlight. They didn't run for office, they built banks and formed a banking trust which controlled virtually all the money available in the United States. These bankers joined the landowners and industrialists in choosing the elected officials. In 1865, after the Civil War, the 13th Amendment to the Constitution gave all <u>men</u> the right to vote, but the Bankers were there behind the scenes using their power (paying) to influence our elected officials to pass bills and laws protecting their interests.

As Thomas Jefferson warned us, today those banking families along with the most powerful politicians and industrialists from North America and Europe ("the corporations that have grown up around the banks") have formed a much more powerful and sophisticated organization that currently commands influence over our government as well as Canada and other nations throughout Europe. They are the Bilderberger Group. The group is comprised of high powered bankers, high ranking politicians and major industrialists from as many as 18 different countries. In recent years, the meetings of the Bilderberger Group have been open to just about everyone and they have invited the press to attend and record them. Why? What better way to dispel doubt and hide what you are doing than to give the appearance of being open and above board. Big Banks and Big Industry have built dynasties based on deceit and corruption while playing to the People. It is the private secret meetings behind closed doors of the core group that make up the plans for financial dominance and control. These are the people that are currently influencing our Governments and running our country.

How did this group gain the power to control these governments? Let's just say for now that we gave it to them. Not necessarily this generation, but our grandparents and great grandparents. What keeps them in power are those who blindly follow the party line or simply vote the single party button on the ballot or don't vote at all or only when we are electing a new president. Essentially, we gave this group the power they wanted and needed to take control of, with little exception, the leading countries of the world.

Representatives to the House are elected every two years, Presidents every four years and Senators every six years. Yes, that's right, we elect Senators for a six-year term. Why are there Senators on the ballot every two years? Because, the Senate is divided into thirds and we elect one third of the Senate every two years. If you only vote in the Presidential elections, you are missing the opportunity to vote out the bulk of the Elected Officials who are ruining your life.

To explain how this power was given and how it has been abused, we should travel back in time, probably to the Revolutionary War, but although I will provide some history, I'm not going to try to explain 225 years of America's history, but I will, however, go back a little over 100 years to 1909.

THE RATIFICATION PROCESS

Although most Americans know at least some of the Constitution and its Amendments, and the basic functions of our government branches, I am listing and briefly defining the most abused as reference. The complete text of the Constitution of The United States of America and its Amendments are included in the Constitution chapter.

The men who drafted the Constitution recognized the document had to withstand the trials of time and built a document that would be very difficult to change; but, they also saw that the Constitution couldn't be so rigid as to prevent change as the nation grew. In fact, they saw a need almost immediately to revise the Constitution.

Most of us know the Constitution was first put into place in 1789 and the first ten amendments to the Constitution were adopted and ratified in 1791 and are known collectively as the Bill of Rights or Liberty Amendments.

What you may not know is that since 1789 there have been approximately 11,500 proposals to amend the Constitution, or that during every two-year session of Congress our representatives in both the House and Senate propose roughly two hundred amendments. Fortunately, most of these proposals do not get passed by the committee where they were proposed and the small fraction that do get passed the committee don't gain enough support in the House or Senate to be submitted to the States for ratification. If the proposal is supported by both houses, it will be submitted to the Supreme Court for Constitutional review before being sent to the States for ratification. The Ratification process sets forth that any amendment to the Constitution must be reviewed and agreed upon by two thirds of the States. _This was how our founding fathers added flexibility into the constitution.

There are a couple of flaws in this process. First there is the assumption the State Supreme Courts and Governments will actively review the proposal. If the states simply rubber stamp the proposal, as some do, then the process can fail and an unconstitutional amendment can be ratified. The second flaw is once a proposed amendment is submitted to the States in the ratification process, neither the House, Senate nor Supreme Court has any control over it and there is no way to call it back from the States or rescind it if it is ratified bypass the required number of States.

Until 1950, the ratification process was monitored by the Secretary of State. From 1950 to 1985 the responsibility was shared between the Secretary of State and the Administrator of General Services. In 1985 this became the sole responsibility of the Archivist. The Archivist is the head of the National Archives and Records Administration (NARA). Both the Secretary of State and NARA fall under the Executive Branch and are the smallest of all Government departments with about the greatest importance. Neither have ever had the time nor staff to read every one of the thousands of documents that flow through their respective offices.

After Congress proposes an amendment and the proposal is submitted to the States, the State Governments and State Supreme Courts are supposed to review the proposal any irregularity or unconstitutionality in the proposed amendment before ratifying it. The only person monitoring the ratification process is the Archivist of the United States and the subordinate Office of the Director of the Federal Register. The Archives receive thousands of documents per day and must categorize and file every one of them as well as maintain those documents on the Archives website. They do not have the staff or the time to read every piece of paper that comes to them. Thus, many times one document is added to another purely by its reference number. This is a major flaw in the ratification of documents. There must be a procedure for recalling the proposal, rescinding it even if ratified if found to be unconstitutional, and a system to ensure steps are followed to keep a document from being presented to the states before having a Judicial Review.

Taxes and the Internal Revenue Service (IRS)

"To compel a man to subsidize with his taxes the propagation of ideas which he disbelieves and abhors is sinful and tyrannical." -- Thomas Jefferson

To fully understand the Constitution and the Amendments you should be aware that, by definition, an Amendment, is a minor change, addition, or correction. It is not a complete voiding of one section to replace it with an Amendment. The first ten Amendments to the Constitution made these minor changes to give us the bill of rights. Likewise, sixteen of the other seventeen Amendments follow the definition of minor change, addition or correction. The 16th Amendment, however, voids the Constitution's sections on taxation and replaces them with the Amendment.

I could have written a complete explanation of each of the Amendments in order, but that would have been exceptionally boring and this book would have sat on the shelf and would never have been read, so I opted to take the Amendments, Bills and Laws in order of greatest abuse of the American People and The Constitution starting with the 16th Amendment.

No one alive in the United States today can remember a time when they weren't paying Federal and State Income Taxes, but it hasn't always been this way.

Article 1, Section 8 of the Constitution gave Congress the right to lay and levy taxes on Business, Imports and Exports to provide income for the Government to pay the nations debts and provide for the National Defense. It also dictated that the bulk of the income from those taxes was to be distributed among the states based on the population or census of the states. It forbade the capitation (taxes on Services) or direct (Taxes on Income) taxation of the people.

In 1861, after the secession of the Southern States from the Union, revenue from Business Exports and Imports was greatly reduced. The costs of financing the Civil War were mounting and with the lack of funds from normal taxation, President Lincoln, understandably, asked Congress to pass a temporary emergency tax on the income of the population of the Union. In the Confederate States, Jefferson Davis instituted a similar tax on income. The Internal Revenue Service was formed and commissioned under the Department of The Treasury in 1862 to monitor and collect these taxes as well as the original taxes from business, exports and imports. The tax rate in 1862 was a flat 3 percent on income between $600 and $10,000 and 5 percent on income over $10,000. After the war, Congress allowed this income tax to remain in place to aid in the reconstruction of the war-torn country. It was allowed to expire in 1872. This was the first time that income was taxed, but not the only time that Congress proposed such a tax. Fact of the matter is the senate and congress had proposed an income tax on individuals almost every year since the Louisiana purchase in 1803. Most of these proposals never passed the review committees and those that did were deemed unconstitutional by the Supreme Court.

In 1894, America was concerned with the prospects of war with Spain and Congress Proposed the Tax Act of 1894 which the Supreme Court Ruled as Unconstitutional so it was not passed into law. There was no more income tax collected until 1914.

In 1908, the Populist movement demanded tax reform and in 1909, a proposal was submitted to change the U.S. Constitution. The difference between this proposal and the other proposals for income taxes was the proposal of 1909 would amend the Constitution where the others were proposed as acts that had to pass judicial review prior to being made law. This new proposal to amend the Constitution had to be ratified by the States.

In 1909, in his address to the 61st Congress, President Taft proposed a 2 percent taxation on corporate income expanding on the constitutional taxation of businesses but not the individual. Several proposals were offered by various Senators and Representatives with the winning proposal being submitted by Senator Nelson Aldrich, the head of the Senate Finance Committee. Keep this name in mind for it comes up again. Aldrich's proposed amendment gave Congress the power to levy taxes on anything they wanted including Income (Direct Tax) and Taxation on Services (Capitation) and to increase or change them as desired without public consent, <u>after all didn't the elected House and Senate representatives have the voice of the people?</u> They may have had our voice but not in our best interests and we now pay tax on top of tax on everything from drinking water to the use of our telephones. Below is a partial list of the taxes levied by Congress without the consent of the people. The Aldrich proposal also allowed the Federal Government to use the taxes at will and no longer had to distribute those tax proceeds to the states. In fact, over the last century since the proposal was adopted as the 16th Amendment, the Federal Government has commonly used the collected Taxes as leverage, bribery and blackmail to make the States conform to certain laws and mandates. An example of this was the mandated 55 miles per hour speed limit that was passed in the 1970s. Not all States wanted to reduce their speed limits. The Federal Government blackmailed the States into conformity by threatening to withhold Federal funds for education, road maintenance and various other programs. The States had no choice but to comply. Withholding Federal funds for highways and education are the most commonly used tactics to ensure State compliance with Federal Government mandates and have been used for everything from drug-free work place laws to removing billboards from the highways. This is money which by the Constitution, lawfully belongs to the States, not a leverage tool for the Federal Government.

As I mentioned, even though all previous attempts to pass income tax laws and acts had been ruled unconstitutional. This taxation proposal was submitted as an amendment to the Constitution meaning that the States would have to ratify it and if ratified would overrule the Supreme Court's ruling. The Proposal passed both houses and was submitted to the Supreme Court and to the States for ratification simultaneously. It was again declared unconstitutional by the U.S. Supreme Court, but ratified by the States.

In the case of the 16th Amendment, the Supreme Court Ruling was just another document filed with the rest of the documents for the proposed Amendment. In 1913, the Office of the Secretary of State collected the ratification documents from the states and added them to the proposal. When they had collected the required number of ratification documents from the States, the Secretary prepared an affidavit of ratification and sent the proposal with all its related paperwork and affidavit to the President for signature into law. Before 1925, there were no time limits in place for ratifying amendments, to put importance on them to get passed. After 1925, time limits to respond or ratify a proposal were placed on the documents and States are normally given seven years to ratify a proposal before it expires. The only control to the ratification process is the seven-year time limit placed on the proposal. The Archivist is not responsible for making sure that the Supreme Court Ruling is adhered to. His only job is to count the ratifying States and to ensure that each document has all its pages when he submits it to the President. Whether the proposal is declared unconstitutional by the Supreme Court or not is inconsequential to the archivist. The Court's decision is simply added to the mounting stack of paper for that reference number.

There needs to be a method of checks for amendment proposals and a method of retrieving or terminating a proposal that is in the ratification process to keep it from making its way to the President's desk. In the case of the 16th Amendment there were no checks and balances. Congress, with questionable ethics, did their job; the Supreme Court did their job; the State Supreme Courts failed to do their job, performing a Judicial Review; The State Government without input from their Court did their job voting to ratify the amendment and the Secretary of State and archivists did their job collecting the ratification documents. The proposal landed on President Taft's desk 3 February 1913 and was signed into law and adopted as the 16th Amendment to the U. S. Constitution. Whether President Taft was aware of the change from his desire to tax corporate income to taxing the individual will never be known, however, the results were not in the best interest of the country and are unconstitutional.

Prior to 1913, the Constitution provided for business imports and exports to be taxed "uniformly throughout the United States". From those taxes the Federal Government was to take a small portion "to pay the Debts and provide for the common Defense and general Welfare of the United States. The remainder of the funds was to be distributed between the states based on their population. There are some groups and individuals that interpret the Constitution's "uniform" tax as a flat tax, and that interpretation is far more accurate than a tax that is delineated by income level and personal deductions. In fact, the Constitution clearly states "No Capitation, or other direct, Tax shall be laid, unless in Proportion to the Census or enumeration herein before directed to be taken". Capitation is the taxation of Services and Direct Tax is a tax on personal income. Government was never supposed to tax the citizens, it was supposed to operate on the taxes raised by the taxation of business imports and exports.

In 1909, the majority party in Congress were the Republicans (remember these Republicans are mostly businessmen who would be opposed to having any further taxation of businesses). They proposed an amendment that would change the lives of the American people for the next 100 plus years. Congress wanted the 16th Amendment to pass, so they sold the State Governments on the benefit of ratifying the amendment. Here's how: The amendment gave the Federal Government the ability to create their own taxes, Direct and Capitation. The States complained that the proposal took away their rightful portion of the federal taxes. Congress gave them a bone to encourage the ratification; Since the Federal Government no longer had to make distribution to the states, this opened the door for State Governments to amend their constitutions to mirror the Federal and could now generate revenue by levying Property, Sales and Income taxes and they could use those taxes as they saw fit and raise them when needed to more money to run the State Government. This naturally trickled down to the County and City Governments. The States jumped on the money train and because there were no checks to let the States know of the Supreme Court Ruling, they ratified the 16th Amendment.

Once the 16th Amendment was ratified, our elected leaders, from all levels of government, were content to do business in whatever manner they saw fit to increase the size of Government and further their personal agendas. The 16th Amendment allowed Federal, State and lower levels of government full authority to abuse our rights and the Constitution.

The most recent of these abuses was in March, 2013 when President Obama passed an Executive Order overriding the Congress imposed Government Wage Freeze by authorizing a .05% raise for himself, the Vice President, Members of Congress and the Senate, and Federal workers. Where did we have any say in that proceeding? We didn't! Although, .05% is a small sum when computed against a $200,000 salary, the fact is that when you tally that percentage across all the Federal workers involved, it becomes a much larger figure that "We, The People," are paying for in taxes and it should be a matter of concern to all of us.

As I mentioned earlier our Representatives propose about 200 amendments to the Constitution during each two-year session of Congress, but most die in the committee process.

It takes 34 States to convene a Constitutional

Convention. States attending a Constitutional Convention may challenge the Federal Government on bills, laws and proposed Constitutional Amendments that impose unlawful burdens upon the citizens of their states. If We, The People, can't get past the Federal Government fortifications to make the changes that best serve us, then we must make our State Governments act on our behalf. But, first we must make the Cities and Counties repeal the doctrine that enabled them to levy taxes. Then collectively, we must repeal the State Constitutional Amendment that allows them to Levy Taxes. The states must then convene a Constitutional Convention to make the Federal Government repeal the 16th Amendment. The 10th Amendment states that the Federal Government possesses only those powers delegated to it by the States or the People through the Constitution. If We, The People think our Government has too much power, **it is up to us to take it away from them.** We have allowed our elected Representatives to pass laws in direct violation of our rights thus giving power to the Federal Government that We, The People didn't condone. In truth, we followed blindly our representatives with the belief they were serving us. We, The People need to vote out those State Representatives, both at the State and Federal level, who seem to be trying to give the Federal Government more power than it needs or deserves by voting in representatives who place the people's rights and interests first. Since the Parties seem to be a large part of the problem, then a partial solution would be not to vote for anyone with a Party affiliation and I mean any Party; Republican, Democrat, Tea Party, it doesn't matter. If a Party is involved, then the minute the representative crosses into the District of Columbia they are all the same. We need to vote for People Not Parties.

The 16th Amendment was one of the first actions where We, The People, have given up our rights to those we elect. In this instance, both our Federal and State legislators failed to serve the best interest of the people and blatantly violated the Constitution of the United States and our right of no taxation without representation. As you can see, there are loopholes and flaws in the system that allow the powerful and power hungry to circumvent our rights for their own greed.

We need to make our Federal legislators propose a well worded Amendment to repeal the 16th Amendment rather than spend their time trying to change the Constitution and let our State legislators know that we want this ratified quickly - Not the 202 years of the 27th Amendment - more like the 6-month time frame of the 12th Amendment. This would be a starting point to stop the abuse and begin to put government back on track as far as limiting taxation and the size of government. If there aren't enough taxes from business, imports and exports to pay the bills then our elected officials would have to Stop Funding Special Interests or take a pay cut. I'm not going to believe or try to make you believe that our Government, with the size of the nation, and current size of Government, can operate on a flat tax solely on businesses, imports and exports. We, the people are going to have to help by continuing to pay direct and capitation taxes for at least the next 10 years. Statistics have proven that Government can operate and reduce some of the nation's debt on a 10% flat tax, but that tax must not be a matter for the people to vote on. That is a 10% tax on every dollar earned by every person or business entity with an income. No deductions, no loop holes to lessen the amount of tax and no refunds.

We should also have a unanimous vote on whether to pass a proposed amendment before the States ratify it. Taxation and changes to our Constitution are not issues to leave up to our politicians, they will always act in favor of their own interests.

I've stated many times that we need to take back control of our government. We need to take measures to make our elected officials, the people we hire to represent us, "Toe the Line". "Toe the Line" is another phrase you will see often throughout this book. It simply means to consciously conform to a standard. That standard being to hold themselves above reproach and to do the job they were hired (elected) for and serve the people of this country, not themselves and not the special interest groups or big banks and big business. Our legislators and other elected officials must be made to remember that they are Civil Servants and work for us, we don't work for them.

Here is a partial alphabetical list of the Direct and Capitation taxes that the House of Representatives have laid since the 16th Amendment became law. Remember before 1913 none of these taxes existed.

Building Permit Tax
CDL License Tax
Cigarette Tax
Dog License Tax
Federal Income Tax

Fishing License Tax
Food License Tax
Fuel Permit Tax
Gasoline Tax
Hunting License Tax
Inheritance Tax
Inventory Tax
IRS Interest Charges (Tax on top of Tax)
IRS Penalties (Tax on top of Tax)
Liquor Tax
Luxury Tax
Marriage License Tax
Medicare Tax
Property Tax
Real Estate Tax
Road Use Tax
Recreational Vehicle Tax
Service Charge Tax
Social Security Tax
Sales Tax
School Tax
State Income Tax
Telephone Usage and Surcharge tax
Utility Taxes (taxes on heating fuels and
electricity)
Vehicle and Marine Craft Taxes
Well Permit Tax

The following are the taxes that were laid on businesses in addition to the constitutional import and export taxes.

Federal Unemployment Tax (added by the Social Security Act of 1934)
State Unemployment Tax (Also added by the Social Security Act of 1934)
Corporate Income Tax
Workers Compensation Tax

This list does not include the many State and Local taxes that we pay.

While I'm about taxes I must bring light about bond issues.

Bond issues are small increases to certain taxes such as property taxes to pay for certain supposed improvements in the community. Here's how bond issues are supposed to work. Bond issues normally have a very specific purpose and length of time. For example, the city wants to build a new library. The cost of the project is estimated at one million dollars. To get the extra money for the project the city proposes a 1% increase to the property tax for five years. If passed by the voters the money is supposed to be placed in an escrow or bond account that draws interest to pay for this project. At the five-year point bids are requested from local businesses to begin work on the project. The additional 1% tax for bond is terminated and property taxes are reduced by that percentage.

When was the last time you saw a reduction in any tax? Rarely, if ever. The city, county and state conveniently find something else that will require a bond continuance for another five years and five years after that and again after that toll we finally tell them <u>NO.</u> Or they just don't ever terminate the bond tax.

Bond issues are the great manipulation of the public's trust. The proponents of a bond issue paint a rosy picture of why we need the projects. Better lighting along roads, library expansion, new community areas like swimming pools, parks etc., public transportation. These are all noble causes, but things our tax dollars should be paying for without adding more taxes.

In recent years, a bond issue was approved by the voters in Albuquerque, NM. This bond was approved for a roadway expansion to relieve bottlenecks in the commuter traffic from the west side of town to east side costing $42 million. The bond tax was never reduced or terminated and without voter approval the city spent an additional $63 million on a baseball complex, a couple of swimming pools, pickle-ball courts, and various other projects. The city claimed that they could use that money for whatever they wanted if they had a two thirds approval from the city council. Excuse me! This is tax payer money that was approved for one project through a bond issue on the ballot. Where did the city get the right to over spend that bond by $63 million of the tax payers' money? If the project was completed $63 million under budget, the extra money should have been returned to the home owners who paid into it in the way of a tax break for the next several years or had the citizens of Albuquerque vote on which projects to spend the money.

This is just one issue in one city, but there are many such issues happening in every bond election in every city, county and state in this country. It needs to stop! Our governments need to be honest when they propose a bond issue and maintain very strict record keeping to ensure when the bonds reach the projection costs and terminate those that have been met. It's not up to our city councils to write blank checks with our taxes or use them for purposes other than what they are intended. If the bond has funds available after the project completion, then it's up to the voters to what project those funds are used. I can think of about a million things in this community that are far more important than pickle-ball courts. For those of you who are not familiar with what pickle-ball is; it is a game like tennis played with a paddle resembling a ping pong paddle and a ball resembling a whiffle ball. I don't know the statistics of how popular this game is or what demographics play it, but I seriously doubt if it warrants 2.5 million tax payer dollars without some type of authorization by the people.

CONGRESSIONAL PAY AND EXPENSES

The Constitution provides that the members of the three branches of government shall receive remuneration or pay for their services while in office. It further stipulates that the President and Vice President, shall not receive an increase or decrease of their pay during their elected term. Meaning that the pay for these two offices can be changed once every four years, but that change won't be effective until after the next election and the newly elected or reelected President and Vice President are sworn into office. There was no mention of pay changes for Congress. Recognizing this oversight, in September 1789 the newly formed Congress of the United States submitted a proposed amendment to the States for Ratification. This proposal holds the record for longest period to be ratified taking 202 years for ratification. It could have been ratified at any point with far less than the 38 states that finally ratified it in May 1992 when it was signed into law as the 27th Amendment to the Constitution.

The 27th Amendment delays laws affecting Congressional Salary from taking effect until after the next election of representatives and restricts Congress from considering any other Congressional pay increase until after the first is in effect, meaning that Congress can only have a change to their pay once every two years.

The 27th Amendment is the most violated Amendment in the Constitution. Since it was ratified in 1992, there have been only two years in which Congress did not pass a Federal Pay Raise that included members of Congress. Almost every year since the passage of the 16th Amendment in 1913, Congress has voted to raise their salary and that includes the twenty-five years following the ratification of the 27th Amendment in 1992. Every one of these raises went into effect the first pay period of the month following passage by Congress, not the month following the swearing in of the Representatives from the next election. Thus, making all the raises since 1992 unlawful and they should be reversed and all the living Representatives (Current, voted out of Office or retired) that have drawn these pay increases should be made to pay back the money that was illegally obtained.

The raise given by President Obama's Executive Order in March of 2013 was a direct violation of the 27th Amendment on two counts. 1) It increased the pay for the Executive Offices **during** the President's term and 2) because it was effective the first pay period of April, 2013 and should not have taken effect until **after** the Election in November, 2014 and **after** newly elected representatives had been sworn into office in **January 2015**. The raise that Congress authorized in 2013 that was effective January 2014 is another violation of the 27th Amendment, because it **should not have even been presented** to Congress for consideration until **after** the March 2013 Executive Ordered raise was in effect and then if passed would not have been effective until after the election of 2016 and those representatives sworn into office in 2017.

There have been two years in which there was a freeze on government wage increases, 2011 and 2012, but as we saw in 2013 either Congress or the President by Executive Order can cancel the freeze and give themselves a raise.

The way Congress gets around the Constitution when passing Federal pay increases is to call them Cost of Living Adjustments or COLA. There have been court cases brought against the Government concerning COLA and the Constitution. These cases, tried in District and Circuit Courts, upheld that Congress could award a COLA increase since it was a temporary adjustment and not a formal raise and not permanent. The cases were submitted to the U.S. Court of Appeals which maintained that this was a constitutional issue and a matter for the U.S. Supreme Court since it is their job, through Judicial Revue, to ensure the Constitutionality of the bills. To date the Supreme Court hasn't heard any of these cases and hasn't ruled on the issue of COLA. Why hasn't the Supreme Court made a ruling? Because ruling COLA as a raise would affect their income since they are paid through the system that otherwise would limit their pay raises to once every two years.

What's the difference between a Raise and COLA? A Raise is considered a permanent increase to a salary, while COLA is an

Adjustment with a temporary meaning; however, since these Congressional COLA increases don't have an expiration date and since the next "Pay Increase" figures these COLA adjustments into the base rate of the raise, they are permanent increases to Federal Pay. If the pay increase is a Cost of Living **Adjustment** it should have an expiration, such as: expires one year after the effective date or before any other pay increase. If there are no time limits or expiration terms, it is a permanent raise and falls under the 27th Amendment. If the Government's COLA is a temporary adjustment, then any "Raise" should be an increase of the salary prior to and without the COLA and the COLA should be deleted from the pay prior to implementing the raise and remain deleted until another COLA adjustment is placed. There should **NEVER** be a raise and COLA passed during the same year or even within two years of each other. The cost of living doesn't increase that fast.

> *Example: if the salary is $1000 per year and a 1% COLA adjustment is given the salary would become $1010. Then a 2% raise is given. If this 2% is based on the salary with COLA, the salary becomes $1030.20 and would make the COLA Adjustment permanent. If the same 2% raise is given on the salary without COLA, the salary becomes $1020. If every representative were paid equally at $100,000.00 (which we all know is not the case) the 2% in the example becomes $2000 per member. Multiply that times the 500 representatives and the total increase annually is one million dollars.*

I used $1000 and $100,000 in this example, but our Representatives make an average of $180,000 per year. The increase in salary with COLA makes the COLA permanent thereby negating the temporary factor of a COLA adjustment. If our Representatives insist that these raises are COLA then their pay should be audited and the raises on top of the COLA should be adjusted out and the Representatives, Past and Present, should have to pay back the difference.

COLA constitutes a raise of Congressional salary regardless of the "temporary" nature and therefore should fall under the restrictions of the 27th Amendment. COLA needs to be considered a raise, period. If we make COLA a separate raise and allow Government to award COLA without regard to the 27th Amendment, then every year, just as they have for the 25 years since signing the 27th Amendment into law, our Congressional Leaders will award themselves a raise and title it a COLA adjustment. Half a percent here, one percent there, it all adds up to an eventual increase in taxes.

After President Obama's Executive Order of February, 2013, the average increase to members of Congress was about $900. Members of the House and Senate now had salaries of $174,900. Senior leaders of the House and Senate now made $194,400. The Speaker of the House; $224,600, Supreme Court Judges; between $213,900 and $223,500 and Circuit and District Judges; between $174,000 and $184,000. The rest of the Federal Employees got a raise of about one half of one percent. The raise for just the 535 members of the House and Senate exceeded $481,500. Who is paying this? **You Are!**

What makes matters even worse is the fact that in January, 2014 our elected officials and government employees where given another 1% pay raise and then put another freeze on Federal wages. The January 2014 raise, by the 27th Amendment, should not have even been presented to Congress until after the 2014 Elected Officials had taken their seats in office and the March 2013 raise was in effect and then would not have been effective until after the Election in November 2016. Here are two instances where the President and Congress violated the Constitution of the United States as both raises increased Congressional and Presidential salaries. We've seen that the wage freeze is simply a ploy to appease the public. The fact is that Government salaries, at least those of our Executive Offices and Congressional Leaders, are supposed to be frozen for four years and two years, respectively, by the Constitution. But, as we've seen, a wage freeze can be overruled at any time by Congress or the President. If our Elected Leaders followed the 27th Amendment they wouldn't have to waste time arguing and voting on a ruling putting the wage freeze into effect, it would already be there by Constitutional law and could not be overruled by either the President or Congress.

Today our Representatives, make a very good living, while many of those they represent are living on wages or retirement incomes that are far below the Federal Low Income Limits, or are living on welfare or on the street.

Now about the Government payroll. Per the Federal Government Office of Personnel Management (OPM), the Federal Government's version of the Human Resources Departments at most companies and businesses in the country, there are three pay scales for Government Personnel. There is one pay scale for the Military and two pay scales for Civil Service -- the General Schedule, GS1-15, and the Executive Schedule, Levels 1-5, Military Officers in the General Officer Grades are in the Executive Schedule. OPM monitors and manages all pay to all personnel working within the Federal Government. Since pay for the Military has its own pay scale and special pays such as combat, sea service and Hazardous Duty, Military pay is managed by the Defense Finance and Accounting Service or DFAS under the direction of OPM and the Department of Defense.

The Highest rate of pay on the Executive Schedule Pay scale is a Level 1 Executive, which is odd since the other two pay scales start with 1 being the lowest level. These Level 1 executives are not only our elected officials, but also the senior level members of the Cabinet and our Government branches, i.e. the heads of the Forest Service, IRS, Bureau of Land Management, Department of Interior and others. As of January, 2014, the pay for these top-level executives is $201,700. Where did the money for these raises come from? Our Federal Taxes. Yes, I know you all knew that, but what you didn't know was that President Obama had issued that Executive order and then Congress approved yet another raise without even mentioning it to us. Even in the State of the Union Address, these raises were very carefully omitted. Congress was also silent. They voiced their opinion about most of the other Executive Orders President Obama signed, why not this one. Because it gave them more money. Why should they have to tell us - after all, the orders were recorded in the Congressional Record and Government Archives that are open to the public? How many people in this country even know they can look up anything that happens in the Congress by going to the archives or the Congressional Record? How many would even know what to look for or what search word to use to research the archives for a certain bill, amendment or Executive Order? How many would look even if they knew? Less than 1% of the population. 300 Million Americans and less than 3 million know what our government is doing on a regular basis. And you wonder why our government thinks of us as sheep. We blindly follow wherever the wolves take us. When a wolf takes a sheep from a flock of sheep, the other sheep will follow the wolf with the stolen sheep for a short distance. Are we Sheep just following the wolf? Even the sheep know when to stop.

On top of the salaries our representatives draw, every time they travel they are paid for their expenses. A Representative can travel first class to a weeklong conference in New York City where they have been invited to be a guest speaker and in many cases, make several thousand dollars plus their travel expenses which may be reimbursed by OPM. How? Although they are only to give a one hour speech on one day of the conference, they can attend the conference for the entire week. They and any staff members they take, are reimbursed for the round trip 1st class airfare and their hotel room for the week. They are also drawing Per Diem which in New York is around $304 per day, multiplied times seven days equals $2128. They will also receive a payment or Speakers Fee from the conference coordinators that could range between $1000 and $100,000 and in some cases the conference also pays for the transportation and lodging, but the representative can't claim the reimbursement since they are not out of pocket for that money, but they can still claim the per diem. If they can accept the Speakers Fee, they should not be reimbursed their expenses and should not be allowed to draw the per diem and their salary should be reduced by seven days since they are not conducting the business that they were elected for while on a personal speaking engagement. How do we determine if the speaking engagement is personal or in the line of duty? If the event coordinator is paying a Speakers Fee and the representative accepts that fee, it's personal. If the Representative is sent or volunteers to speak about an issue of public interest at no cost to the event, it's Government Business or line of duty. Congressman Loebsack of Iowa frequently visits his district. When he is on these trips he often talks with his constituents and has even removed his jacket worked shoulder to shoulder with the folks in the district. He has worked with farmers, city workers, industry workers and several others. Not all the people he helps have great and glorious jobs. Mucking out a pig, horse or cattle stall is not very prestigious, but he has done it. When he files his travel after returning to Washington, he doesn't include his travel around the district, although, he is entitled to because he is performing the job for which he was hired.

Now, if some representative travels to his home state to attend the birthday party for one of their constituents, during the party they spend time talking to the constituent and people at the party about a certain bill. Is this a reimbursable business trip or is it a personal trip? If the representative is making stops throughout his district or state getting opinions on an issue from the people in the district and happens to stop at the constituents' birthday party while in the area, its business. But if the birthday party is the prime reason for the visit to the district and no other visits to the district are performed, it's personal. We should not be paying for the personal activities of our representatives. Yet, we do it every day.

Here's an example: You are an employee of Company A. If the Company sends you somewhere to either speak to a group on the new innovations the company is working on, the company will reimburse you for your expenses on the trip. But, if you travel to your child's graduation from college and speak at their fraternity or sorority about careers with your company, because your Child asked you to, the expenses are yours to bear because you are there for the graduation not a company function. Our Representatives must be held to that same standard. If it's personal it's their expense, if it's line of duty then they can be reimbursed if there are no other benefits (Speakers Fees) associated with the line of duty travel.

For many months prior to the elections, our representatives are drawing a salary for being our representative, however, they are not doing anything for us. They are out Campaigning for reelection. If they are going to campaign they should take unpaid vacation time or a leave of absence from their position. They should not be paid for representing us while they are trying to further their own career. They should be paying their own way to reelection. We were not paying them when they ran the first time, why should we be paying for any reelection attempt.

What's the solution to keep government wages and our representatives in check?

First, we must Correct the illegal pay raises from the past 25 years and make the representatives that collected them pay the money back or face prosecution for embezzlement.

Second, all Federal employees regardless of position are the same, they work for us. From the President to the lowest General Schedule (GS) employee, these people are ALL, Civil Servants. Therefore, all their wages should be reflected in the General Services Pay Scale. We need to assess what these high-level executives are doing to earn their six figure salaries. Many positions have no responsibility, have no subordinates whom they supervise and have no authority in any decision-making process. What warrants their 6-figure salary? This is a question that must be answered by our elected leaders.

With exception to the Military, we must make Government

employees conform to a single Pay Scale which is set out in The General Schedule, after all they are all Civil Servants. The General Schedule consists of 15 Graded Positions which are further broken down into steps. Step 1 is the starting step for the grade and 2 is the first promotion after a year of service. The other 8 steps are basically raises at 2 year increments of service. If the top-level person of the current GS pay scale at GS-15 Step 10, started their career eighteen years ago, as a GS-1 their base pay would be approximately $130,810 a year.

If we take the basic GS pay scale and add GS Levels up to GS-22, the scale would cover all the executive schedule levels plus the Vice-President and President. Each of the new Grades would have a wage base 2% higher than the preceding level. For instance, a GS-16 would be those personnel currently in Level 5 of the Executive Schedule and the annual pay for those people would be $133,426 per year. Currently, a Level 5 person on the Executive Schedule makes $147,200 per year. If there was only one person in this grade, we would have just saved the country $14,000 per year. The Vice-President currently makes $234,219. Using the pay scale presented above, the Vice-President would be classified into the GS-21 pay rate, making his salary $147,313, a savings of $86,906. Imagine how much we can save by holding all the Government to this standard pay scale. Even if the pay scale had a 5% increase between levels, the savings to the country would be enormous. Based on the chapter on Homesteading and limiting the terms of Congress, Senate and Judges there would be a maximum of 5 steps for grade levels GS-16 through GS-20, since we need to hold to a ten-year maximum term of office, and 3 steps for GS-21, the Vice-President and GS-22, the President, since these two positions have terms of only eight years maximum. Pay for GS 21 and 22, the Executive Offices, could only be changed every four years per the Constitution regarding Presidential remuneration. Pay for GS 16 through 20 could only be changed every two years in accordance with the 27th Amendment.

Elected Officials would be awarded vacation and leave time based on the OPM Schedule and would have to be requested just as our other Civil Servants are required to do.

Travel is authorized for Business only. If a Representative receives fees for speaking engagements, they are not authorized to claim or accept payment for travel or per diem and their salary will be reduced by the number of days on the junket unless they take accumulated vacation. When campaigning for reelection the time will be deducted from their accumulated vacation time and once they have used all their vacation, they are either back to work or on an unpaid leave of absence.

Third, the Military Pay scale would remain separate and independent due to the unique special pays, i.e. combat, hazardous duty and sea duty pay, but should be changed to include all Officer Grades including the Generals and Admirals. The Military Pay Schedule should be raised to reflect at least the minimums of the GS schedule. Currently a GS-1 step-1starting salary is $25,597 per year while an E-1 in the Military starting salary is $19,200 per year. Both salaries taken from 2017 pay scales.

The Articles of the 27th Amendment should be enforced, but should be amended to include all Government employees.

THE RIGHT TO BEAR ARMS

"No free man shall ever be debarred the use of arms." - Thomas Jefferson

Since I mentioned the Second Amendment earlier, it's time to put my two cents in on that subject.

The Constitution grants us the right to keep and bear arms and yet the Government is forever trying to prevent us from exercising that right. Many States have gone so far as to ban guns by the nomenclature of the weapon i.e. if a rifle has a pistol grip style stock it is illegal. I don't advocate keeping automatic weapons or weapons of mass destruction and agree that some of this type of weapon should be strictly for the military and law enforcement.

Although we have been attacked by terrorists on occasion, our enemies have never tried to put soldiers on the mainland of the United States. The reason for that is they believe behind every American door is a weapon. The fact that we can arm ourselves puts a weapon behind almost every door and those who don't have a weapon can probably borrow one from a neighbor if it was needed.

One problem with Gun Control is, it is a double-edged sword. Those who defend Gun Control believe guns are instruments of domination, lawlessness and terrorism, while those who oppose Gun Control believe guns made us free and will keep us free.
Depending on the hand wielding the sword of gun control, both beliefs are correct. Criminals, anarchists and terrorists use guns for control, domination and crime. While the honest person uses guns to protect their family, home and property.

The debate will continue forever, but the fact is and I quote President Ronald Reagan. "If there are guns, the individual that wants a gun for a crime is going to have one and going to get it. The only person who's going to be penalized and have difficulty is the law-abiding citizen, who then cannot have [it] if he wants protection -- the protection of a weapon in his home." We are punishing honest folks who keep arms for the deeds performed by criminals.

Articles in the paper about children being killed after finding loaded weapons in cars, purses or unsecured around the home give fuel to the debate. Gun control opponents will argue that it's not the gun that killed, it's the person holding it. Since many of these shootings are accidental, perhaps the problem isn't in controlling the gun but in educating the people who buy them including how to care for them and how to secure them away from their children. Prior to roughly 1959, high schools across the country offered elective classes for proper use, care cleaning and storage of weapons. Maybe this should be a mandatory class for all students. We have mandatory Sex Education classes at the pre-teen level to prevent unwanted teen pregnancies; but we don't have any type of education to prevent children from picking up a gun. Gun security is essential, just putting the weapon on a top shelf of a closet will not prevent or deter a child from gaining access. Well-constructed Gun Safes and the education of gun owners and the children who might be exposed to guns is a better deterrent to accidental killings than making and passing laws.

Governments who want to control the people or distrust the people control guns. The first thing Hitler's Nazi Party did in 1935 was gather the guns of private citizens. The Russians also collected the guns of private citizens as the Communists created the Soviet Union. Even in the pre-revolutionary war, England sought to limit and control guns and the amount of shot (bullets) available to the colonists. Yet when the war broke out every American Colonist who could take up arms against the British had a weapon and all the shot and powder they could carry. Because of that we won our independence. The people who were not opposed to their Governments could retain their weapons but had to have them registered with the state and were regularly inspected and interrogated to reevaluate their patriotism to the party and to ensure the weapon was still in their possession. Those early American Colonists could obtain and hide their weapons and shot regardless of laws prohibiting them. The same is true today, if a person wants a gun, there are avenues to obtain them. An example of this would be that the Native American Indians during the Indian Wars could get rifles and ammunition through black market gun runners who profited greatly from the sale of guns to the Indians

The solution: Stop the fight for Gun Control and start the fight to educate gun owners and bring very strong penalties against those who use them for criminal activity. Get tough on Crime. California used to advertise "Use a Gun, Go to Jail." The entire Nation should practice that policy, only let's put it a bit blunter. Use a Gun, spend the rest of your life in a 10 x 10 cube with no outside contact, no exercise yard, and no luxuries of any kind. We aren't going to stop violent crime by punishing the non-criminals by forcing Gun Control. We are going to stop crime by no longer tolerating it and molly coddling the criminals. If the American Civil Liberties Union (ACLU) wants to deal humanely with these criminals maybe they would like to house them. I know of very few crime victims that would be opposed to putting major criminals on a one-way space flight with no brakes into orbit around the sun. For all minor crimes reinstitute the chain gangs and work farms. The proposition of swinging a 20-pound sledge hammer breaking rocks every day for several years might tend to make people think before committing a crime. Stop beating up on the Arizona Sheriff for making prisoners live in tents and wear pink prison suits. What he's doing is working to curb crime in his county.

The Constitution prohibits cruel and unusual punishment, so the "sun" thing wouldn't work. We need to educate gun owners and Criminals should be punished. Take away the big screen TV, the internet access, and recreation and make them live in the cell with two fifteen minute trips to the exercise yard each day where all they can do is follow the inmate in front of them walking a circle around the perimeter.

Gun Control isn't the answer. The solutions I've offered here may not be the answer either, but at least they may be a deterrent to some percentage of the problem. Unfortunately, "Kids will be Kids" and curiosity will overrule all other rules and "Criminals will be Criminals" who could care less about any rules.

"The strongest reason for the people to retain the right to keep and bear arms is, as a last resort, to protect themselves against tyranny in government." - Thomas Jefferson

CITIZENSHIP

"Give me your tired, your poor, your huddled masses yearning to breathe free, the wretched refuse of your teeming shore. Send these, the homeless, tempest-tossed to me, I lift my lamp beside the golden door!" – The New Colossus poem by Emma Lazarus – placard inside the Statue of Liberty.

The 14th Amendment was added to the Constitution in 1866 and sets forth the rules for Citizenship in the United States. It establishes the definition of citizenship and contains clauses for citizenship, immigration and naturalization policies and processes, privileges, immunities and due process.

The debates between the Southern Democrats and Northern Republicans over citizenship were mostly concerning the newly freed slaves in the post-civil war reconstruction period and whether these people should be considered citizens for voting purposes. In the end, Congress drafted a proposed document that was amicable to both sides - a compromise of sorts that both parties felt was a surrender of values, but had enough broad meaning to appease them.

There have been numerous court cases regarding the depth, latitude and wording of the amendment and most have been ruled in favor of the complainant; meaning that the court ruled in favor of the person attempting to gain citizenship. The biggest flaw with the 14th Amendment is that the wording in most of the clauses is so broad as to be subject to interpretation. The meaning of the clause is solely dependent on who is reading it. One hundred people reading the amendment can have a possible one hundred different opinions as to what it says.

The original 14th Amendment was signed into law in a time when there were no "illegal" or "undocumented" immigrants. It wasn't until 1892, almost thirty years later, that immigrants to the United States had to enter through specific ports of entry like the one at Ellis Island. Even after we established the need to register those entering the country, the 14th Amendment wasn't changed to further clarify citizenship. Although our immigration policies have changed based on the interpretation of the 14th Amendment; Congress has never formally defined what citizenship is.

The 14th Amendment reads that any person born in the United States is a Citizen. There have been debates in Congress concerning "Birth Tourism" where a pregnant woman can enter the United States and have her baby born here, making the baby a citizen. The policy in place makes it nearly impossible to deport the parents. Because of our humanitarian nature, we don't condone the separation of a child from its parents. Also, under current policy, the only way to lose citizenship is by either voluntarily voiding citizenship in favor of another or due to having issued fraudulent statements during the naturalization process, or if you have incited armed insurrection or rebellion against the Government. Congress has never drafted a bill that would prevent "Birth Tourism" by making it necessary that at least one parent be a citizen. Most of the other countries of the world have that requirement for a child to be considered a citizen. We Don't. To further this fault, there have been no laws drafted that determine the citizenship of a child born to "illegal" or "undocumented" parents. The same solution of requiring one parent to be a citizen applies here.

In November, 2014, President Obama, in an Executive Order, gave amnesty to nearly 5 million "undocumented" immigrants many of whom had entered the country illegally years before. The Nation and Congress were shocked and appalled by such a blatant and apparent violation of the 14th Amendment. Although I didn't personally care for President Obama, he was within his right to create such an order. Many of those who were given amnesty had children that were born in the United States and had established community ties.

We are using a document that is 160 plus years old and has never been amended from its original purpose, which was to establish the citizenship of the slaves freed by the "Emancipation Proclamation" which gave us a guideline to begin documentation of immigrants in 1892, but has not been given any kind of tune-up since. Times have changed. The national climate has changed. The threat to National Security has changed. Yet we continue to be guided by a document that does not reflect the current United States citizenry.

What's the solution? I've stated it a couple of times.

Congress must redefine citizenship requiring that for a child to be a citizen they must have at least one parent who is a citizen, or undergo the naturalization process.

In many countries, the penalty for illegally entering the country is death or a sentence of life in servitude, for they are considered invaders. There is no court, these people have none of the rights afforded citizens. Some countries immediately deport those who have entered the country illegally, again there are no courts, and these undocumented people are not citizens and, therefore, have no rights of due process. If they come back into the country illegally they face imprisonment or death.

We, as I have mentioned, are a humane people and give rights to everyone, but in regards to citizenship, we need to make a stand. We can no longer allow "illegal" or "undocumented" immigrants to invade this country then demand to share in the rights for which we have fought or the benefits we have worked and contributed to.

Undocumented immigrants should not be allowed to draw social security, welfare or any government supported subsidies. The should not be allowed to obtain State Driver's licenses or be eligible for any Government aid. If their church wants to offer subsidies, that is entirely on the church.

We used to issue fines and close businesses which were found to be hiring undocumented workers. We need to start enforcing those regulations again. There is a requirement for everyone in the workplace to prove their right to work. In every place I have worked I have had to show my social security card and a picture identification. Where are those requirements to draw welfare and social security?

Those who wish to enter this country through legal channels, swear allegiance, and become citizens are welcome. The rest need to be dealt with harshly enough to reinforce the idea that they are not welcome.

Another humane option would be to require those who wish to enter this country to join the Armed Forces. Serve this country for four years on active duty and four years in the Reserve. During this enlistment, they can work toward getting their citizenship.

That brings us to another problem. The current citizenship requirements are so broad that a normal person cannot hope to pass the test. I helped my young enlisted personnel who wanted to become citizens in order to reenlist study for their citizenship exams. Most of the citizens of this country don't know nor are they required to know the information required to pass those tests. The citizenship test requires the person to know all fifty states in both alphabetical order and by date of accession statehood. Most of our citizens can't tell you when their own home state became a state. The person wishing to become a citizen must also be able to list the Presidents in order with their Vice-Presidents and list all 535 members of Congress and the States they represent. To top it off the only language the test is given in is English. Most Visa are issued for two to five years. Two years to learn English, memorize all the required information and perform an act of loyalty to the United States. Could you do this? It isn't any wonder that we have so many people undocumented in the country.

THE ELECTORAL COLLEGE

The 12th Amendment establishes the process by which we elect our President. Earlier I said that you can't blame the country's problems on one party or the other. I say that because the only President who didn't belong to a Party was George Washington and he was not elected by the people, but appointed by the Continental Congress through an electoral system. Washington accepted the Honor of being the new nation's first President, basically because no one else wanted the job and he was the Commander and Chief of the Continental Army. Throughout our country's history, forty-five men have served as President. Washington, as stated had no party. There was one Federalist Party, four Democratic-Republicans, four Whig party and two National Union party, most of whom were elected by a caucus of electors and the two houses of congress **not the people**. Of the other thirty-three Presidents, fifteen were Democrats and eighteen were Republicans. Therefore, leadership of our Government has been an even split between the two parties. Thus, you can't put the blame for the Country's problems on just one party.

Until 1866 the only people who could vote were land owners. Naturally it stands to reason that the only people who could hold office were also land owners. In 1866, the 15th Amendment was passed that gave every man the right to vote but only men who were older than twenty-one years of age. In 1920 Women were given voting rights by the 19th Amendment and in 1971 the voting age was reduced to eighteen by the 26th Amendment. Now all persons over the age of eighteen can vote, but what is our vote worth?

Here is another factor that we, the people have no control over, and another area where the Government has stagnated. Have you ever wondered why we can't get rid of the antiquated electoral system? The system helps keep the powerful in power. How? Each state has a certain number of electors. This number is equal to the number of Representatives and Senators of each State. This number is multiplied by the number of candidates. Each party has its own electors, you have Democratic electors, Republican electors and if there are Independent, Tea, or Green Party candidates on the ballot each of those will have their own set of electors. New Mexico, for instance, has three Representatives and two Senators giving the State Five Electors. If there are three candidates for president, a Republican, a Democrat and a Green Party, each candidate would have five Electors, but not the same five as the other candidates.

The Electors are supposed to keep track of the popular vote and then cast the state's electoral votes for the candidate who wins the popular vote. Unfortunately, these Electors aren't elected, governed or monitored by us and vaguely monitored by the state government. They are appointed by the political parties, each party having their own unique slate of potential Electors.

Electors generally hold a leadership position in their party or are chosen to recognize years of loyal service to the party. This is not to say that the Electors will be in favor of the candidate. Each vote that is cast for a candidate also votes for the virtually invisible Electors. There are a few states which list the Electors beneath the names of the candidates on the ballot.

The College of Electors or Electoral College is a good system as far as it hasn't been corrupted by our politicians. The reason I say that it is a good system is because it attempts to put all the states on an even playing field. If you consider the populations of states like California, New York, Florida, Texas, and Illinois in comparison to states like Wyoming, North and South Dakota, Montana and New Mexico it would be very easy to control who was elected President by sheer volume of population. The Electoral College puts all the states basically on the same footage. That footage isn't quite even but it's closer than population. If enough of the lesser populated states vote for the same candidate, they could cast more electoral votes than the higher populated states. Under the current Electoral system, a candidate must receive 270 electoral votes to win the election. The problem is that a candidate can receive the required 270 electoral votes from just the eleven most populous states and not have to win another state to be elected. Where is the balance? Where is the voice of the remaining thirty-nine States? It would make no difference in the outcome of the election if those 39 states voted together opposite of the big 11 to make an impact on the election. This was epitomized in five Presidential elections when John Q. Adams, Rutherford B.

Hayes, Benjamin Harrison, George W. Bush and Donald Trump lost the "Popular Vote" but won the election based on the Electoral College. If the election were based solely on popular vote, all the lesser populated states together could never out vote the higher population states.

The Electoral College does, to some degree, level the playing field for the lesser populated states but still needs to be tuned to the current status of the country and must be continually refined as the country changes.

Supposedly, the winning candidate (by popular vote) is awarded all the state's Electors, however, there are no Constitutional provisions or Federal laws that require Electors to vote in accordance with the popular vote. For instance, the Electors are generally bound by two pledges, to the popular vote and to their party affiliation, but this varies state to state. Some states bind them to vote the popular vote, while other states bind them to their pledge to their party affiliation, while some don't bind them to anything at all. For simplicity, let's look at Washington D.C. which has three Electors. If two would rather see the opposing candidate, say a Democrat, in office rather than their own party candidate, but the third is for their Republican candidate, the electoral votes could be given to the Democrat rather than the Republican who won the popular vote. If they are pledged to their party, then the Elector vote would go to the Republican. There are no enforceable laws that say they must hold to their pledge.

This was exemplified during the 2016 election, in which there were a record number of defections in the electors. Seven electors cast votes opposing their party's candidates.

Maine and Nebraska have a proportional distribution of electors. The State retains two electors and each congressional district receives one elector. They are trying to maintain some control over the way their electoral vote is cast and trying to ensure that the popular vote is awarded the states electors.

Remember: There are no rules that force them to cast the state's electoral vote with the popular vote.
The only way to make the Electoral College work efficiently is to give each State only five electors and the District of Columbia three electors. Not the five per candidate of the current system, but only five for each State. These Electors should be appointed by the State Governor and the appointment should not be tied to their position in any Party.

Electors should be drawn from the States general population much like jurors are selected. Five people randomly selected from the registered voters. To be fair and insure the absence of bias, there should one elector selected from each party affiliation or non-affiliated person. Everyone must be bound to vote with the popular vote regardless of personal party or opinion about the candidates. After all, it should not be the electors that control the outcome of the election, but the popular vote. This would bring into balance the overbalance of the heavily populated states that have many congressional districts. If an elector votes contrary to the popular vote, they must be held accountable and criminally prosecuted with severe jail time. In the case of a tie or each candidate having the popular vote in exactly twenty-five States, the tie would be broken by the popular vote of the three electors of Washington, D.C. Remove the current criteria requiring a candidate to have 270 electoral votes and make it so they must have the majority of the electoral vote. Even if that Majority is only 3 votes.

The last thing to consider, although not likely, would be that through some legal loophole our legislators have passed in previous decades, the vote can be voided or over-ruled by some Congressional act.

The following is a good example about how the voting process can be usurped by our Government. This happened in 2012 on a city bill that was presented to the voters. A bill was introduced to raise the minimum wage of the city's general population. The vote was soundly unanimous in favor of raising the minimum wage. After the vote, the Mayor and City Council vetoed the bill and voided the vote. There was some small amendment in the city's charter that allowed them to change the outcome of the election to suit whatever purpose they wanted. The city's residents were outraged, but there was nothing they could do about it.

Just because you vote, doesn't mean that you have any control over who or what you are voting for. It only means that you are voicing your opinion. Please, don't misunderstand me. I'm not saying not to vote or not to continue voting. Quite the contrary, Vote and keep voting. Vote in every election, but make your vote count. The purpose of this book as I stated in the forward is to make government accountable and responsible to us. Stand up, speak up and take control of our government. Make it once again a government OF, BY and FOR THE PEOPLE. Make your representatives "toe the line". DON'T follow the party line just because it's how you are registered to vote or the way your family has always voted and DON'T just vote the whole party box just because it's easy.

LAWS, REGULATIONS, ACTS, BILLS AND MANDATES

"Much indeed to be regretted, party disputes are now carried to such a length, and truth is so enveloped in mist and false representation, that it is extremely difficult to know through what channel to seek it. This difficulty to one, who is of no party, and whose sole wish is to pursue with undeviating steps a path which would lead this country to respectability, wealth, and happiness, is exceedingly to be lamented. But such, for wise purposes, it is presumed, is the turbulence of human passions in party disputes, when victory more than truth is the palm contended for." – George Washington

Every time one of the documents contained in this chapter is passed by Congress or the Senate and signed into law by the President. It is up to the Federal Agencies who have responsibility for regulating the documents which pertain to their department. These Agencies create their own regulations and mandates based on how they interpret the bill passed by our Congressional leaders. The Federal Register is a daily report of all these actions and some Agency regulations change frequently. The best example of these Agency actions is the Clean Air Act.

I indicated earlier that most of our Democratic leaders are lawyers. Lawyers as a rule want to litigate everything and are always on the side of their clients doing their best to win over the opposition. The question is, who are the clients of these lawyers? I will tell you that we, the people are the opposition. I also indicated earlier that most of our Republican leaders are businessmen. Businessmen are always trying to sell you something. What are these representatives trying to sell us?

We are all aware of the fact that Government quite frequently proposes bills for different Laws, Regulations and Mandates and often these proposals won't get passed without adding several different riders to them. The Federal Omnibus Bill that gets passed every year is supposed to be a budget document, setting up the federal budget and procurement requirements for the next year, but it has become a forum for everything from African fruit flies to gun control to protecting the vertical stripped Zebra. This is an exaggeration, of course, but if you were to read one of the recent Omnibus Bills you would find that it contains everything but the proverbial kitchen sink. I have yet to understand why, if there is a healthcare bill being proposed, it is necessary to have a gun control, oil pipeline, abortion or same sex marriage rider on it to get it passed by the other Party. Or if a gun control issue is being voted on why a healthcare rider is added so it will pass.

Mandates are something else. Government consistently issues mandates as regulations for different issues. Pollution controls on factories is a worthwhile mandate, but let's be real and honest. Global Warming is considered a Myth perpetrated by the environmental special interest groups and tagged by our Government to force conformity to the pollution regulations by industry. The truth is we needed and still need to clean up air quality. Using Global Warming as the reason is absurd. Just tell it like it is! We cannot breathe bad air! If there is a trend toward any type of global temperature change it's because the world has seasons like we have winter, spring, summer and autumn, but the earth's clock is far different from ours and earth's summer may last decades or even centuries instead of months.

A poor-quality mandate was when Government mandated cigarette manufacturers put a fire retardant in cigarettes. First, the long-term effects of smokers inhaling the retardant was not sufficiently researched, which is one reason the cigarette companies refused to add it to cigarettes until it was researched or it was mandated. Second, the added retardant is a failure. Whether a cigarette burns is in direct relationship to environmental conditions, like fuel availability and air flow. I have been a smoker and I've found that a fire safe cigarette (FSC) is just as likely to burn all the way to the filter lying in an ashtray or on a carpet in a drafty or well ventilated area as it is to burn while being smoked. The statistics show a twenty-one percent reduction in the smoking material fires between 2003 and 2010. Okay, but what changed? There are less smokers. There are better materials in our carpets, furniture, and clothing. In 2010, there were 90,800 smoking material fires. In 2011, there were 90,000 such fires, not much of a significant change. The statistics lump all smoking material together, cigarettes, pipes, cigars, marijuana and other drugs, and the lighters used. Where is the fire safety in the other legal tobacco products? Fire Safety standards do not apply to pipes or cigars. The statistics also do not consider the amount of moisture or precipitation. For instance, a very arid location is more likely to go up in flames than an area that has plenty of humidity or rain. There is a greater chance of a house fire in the winter when furnaces are drying the air than in the summer when evaporative coolers and air conditioners are humidifying the air. I am not disputing that FSC doesn't do some good. There have been FSC cigarettes for about fifteen years and although there may have been a reduction in house and forest fires caused by smoking, there is no evidence or research that would indicate that this reduction is not the result of smokers just being more careful.

A statistic not addressed in the FSC reports is lung cancer, emphysema or chronic obstructive pulmonary disease (COPD). Since the Fire Safe Cigarette mandate, there has been no research into the effects of the retardant on people. We see research on the effects of second hand smoke and cigarettes in general but nothing related to the chemicals and other treatments which make up the fire retardant in fire safe cigarettes. It would be interesting to see the lung cancer statistics for the period of time from 2003 to 2010.

Congress apparently has nothing better to do than sit on their tails and pass laws on the ridiculous. In 1904, instead of spending his time reviewing bills that were under consideration by the House of Representatives, the Speaker of the House found it more important to issue a mandate to the manager of the House Cafeteria requiring that "Senate Bean Soup" be served every day in the House Restaurant. Mandates of this type are still abundant and totally unnecessary in Congress. Who cares about whether "Senate Bean Soup" is on the menu or even served at all in the Congressional restaurants.

Here's my solution to the redundancy of Government Bills, Laws, Regulations and Mandates.

1. Form a Review Panel consisting of 2 Judge Advocate General (JAG) Attorneys from each of the Military Services and about 10 People, from all walks of life, and from each State, 508 members total and provide them conference rooms in either the House or Senate.

2. Provide each member of this Review Panel either a computer with read only access to the documents or a hard copy of each document. (The computer works best; the cost of paper would be exorbitant.)
3. As the members of the Review Panel read each document, the JAG attorneys would be there to answer questions about the meaning of all the legalese.
4. If a Document no longer pertains to the current situation in the U.S., the Document number would be recorded and Congress could vote to have it withdrawn or rescinded from the law.
5. If a document contains riders that do not pertain to the subject of the document, it would be mandatorily removed from law. Congressional vote would be only a formality.
6. If a document contains language that, even with JAG assistance, cannot be understood by most of the Review Panel, then it too would be mandatorily removed from law. If We, the People cannot understand it how can we be expected to follow it?
7. Omnibus Bills, which are usually a conglomerate of anything Congress wants, can only be used for procurement of services and establishing the Federal Budget. Any other use must be considered a violation of the human and civil rights of the people.
8. If a document is over 200 pages long it should be mandatorily removed from law. Our Congressional representatives receive many documents during each session of Congress. The longer the document, the less chance there is that it was read by those persons who vote it into law. Representatives read the cover summary which is usually several pages then decide whether to vote for or against the bill.
9. Congress must stick to the task at hand – Representing the People of The United States. **Toeing the Line!**

Most people can change a subject, express a view on a subject or start a topic of conversation in a sentence. If everyone in Congress including the cabinet, and department heads were to write one paragraph in a bill, the bill wouldn't exceed 200 pages. In this book, I have identified the problems, offered solutions, given my opinion and references and expanded these with examples and instances and still have less than 250 pages. If I had defined every word in this book every time it occurred, I would be unable to fill 10,000 pages. Most popular authors create spellbinding novels in less than 1000 pages and a 200-year history of the U.S. Marine Corps takes less than 200 pages. Why does our Government think it takes 10,000 or more pages to draft a law or bill that the people of the United States must follow? What are they trying to hide in all the rhetoric on those pages? You can be assured that whatever it is, it is not in our best interest.

THE SOCIAL SECURITY ACT
AND WELFARE

"The democracy will cease to exist when you take away from those who are willing to work and give to those who are not."- Thomas Jefferson

I hope that in the first chapters you have found reason to evaluate your elected leaders and to change the perception that they are working in our best interest. Although, most of these chapters have dealt with what our Government has been doing over the past century, the fact is that unless we act and do something now, they will continue the abuse of the American people; and, in the future, our children and grandchildren will not be afforded the luxuries or benefits of freedom that this country was founded on.

Our Representatives in both the Senate and the House of Representatives have continually revised, changed and amended most bills to the point where finding the original document is a task. Reading through the mountainous volumes of added script from amendments, the original meaning becomes so convoluted by add-ons you wonder if you are still reading the same document or what document you are reading. There are Chapters, Sections, Clauses and paragraphs that never reference the bill they pertain to or the purpose for which they were written. Some of these clearly violate the Constitution and the Bill of Rights, while others contradict the information given by the preceding document. That is especially true of documents that have been subject to changes by every President since their inception. The Social Security Act is one such piece of legislation.

The Social Security Act was passed and signed into law in August of 1935 under President Franklin D. Roosevelt (D) as part of the "Second New Deal" policy. It is widely believed that the act was established expressly for supporting the elderly after retirement. Those funds contributed under the Federal Insurance Contributions Act or FICA taxes were to be placed in a special account for this purpose and those funds were later added to the general fund. This was not true in 1935 and is no truer today. It would be nice to believe that if we just put the FICA into a private investment account we could save the program, but unfortunately that isn't going to happen.

The Social Security Act was designed to fail from the very beginning. No one in Congress looked at the long-term condition of having all the Welfare burden placed on the shoulders of the working class or a division of funds to insure the longevity of the Act. In 1935 the world was immersed in the greatest global depression in history. Millions were out of work and families were starving. Congress considered Welfare a temporary aid while people looked for work, not visualizing that the future would produce a whole subculture of people who relied solely on Welfare for their existence – Nor did they envision a situation where the system would be so out of control that a person could make more on welfare than they do working. The Social Security Act was the first act of Socialism established by our Government. In fact, many of the Congressmen who opposed the act asked openly "Isn't this Socialism?" From the date, it was enacted in 1935 to the present day, the fund has provided money to the States to support Welfare, Unemployment, Aid to Dependent Children, Poverty Assistance, housing subsidies, utility subsidies, cell phones, worker compensation for injury and the State personnel to administer these programs. All of this was in addition to the support of Social Security for the elderly. Social Security, because of the ties to welfare, was never supposed to succeed in anything more than creating a Welfare State, "Socialism." Welfare does exactly what Thomas Jefferson described. It takes away from those who are willing to work and gives it to those who are not. Those who saw the problem in 1935 were appeased by a commitment to place all the surplus funds received from the FICA taxes into a special fund and invested in both marketable and non-marketable securities for Social Security retirement benefits for the elderly who had contributed to the plan. Unfortunately, the account was set up but Social Security has rarely had enough surplus to invest to prolong the programs' life span. Money from other Federal taxes have been channeled into the Social Security Trust Fund to keep it active, and in the few times when the fund did have a surplus, the money that had come from other sources was repaid. Government has been borrowing from Peter to Pay Paul for the last 80 years and today with Federal debt in the Trillions (Trillion that's 1000 Billion) of dollars it is becoming increasingly more difficult to maintain the program.

Here's the problem, NO FICA taxes were collected before 1937. In 1937, there were already people who were retirement age, but had never contributed a penny in FICA. Example the first Social Security Retiree retired one day after Social Security started. His total contribution to the plan was five cents, his lump sum check from Social Security was seventeen cents. Another retired after three years of paying into FICA. Her total contribution was $24.75. Her benefit amount was $22.54 per month and she lived to be 100 years old and had collected $22,888 in social security benefits.

Nineteen thirty-seven, in addition to being the starting year for FICA, was also the first year that death benefits were paid - approximately 53,000 of them. The "Death Benefit" payment in 1937 was to be a lump sum survivor's benefit to offset the lack of FICA payments into Social Security. I could not find a definitive source, it is very difficult to determine the amount of these initial benefits, however, they probably weren't very much. Originally the "Death Benefit" figure was supposed to be approximately 3.5% of the total amount contributed, but as Social Security lost revenue because of the multitudes on welfare, the amount was reduced to a flat $255.

In 1937, FICA taxes were about 2% of a person's wages of which the employer paid half. In 2014, FICA taxes are 12.4% of which the employer still pays half. FICA is what is called a regressive tax, meaning that the more you make the less you pay. Tell me this wasn't set up by the rich and powerful. To make matters even worse, in November, 2014, President Obama issued an Executive Order granting amnesty to over 5 Million people that were in the United States illegally most of whom could not get Welfare in the past and now can.

Federal statistics show that in 2009, nearly 51 million Americans received $650 billion in Social Security benefits. Approximately $12,745.10 per year per person living on Social Security Retirement or Survivors benefits. If you were to take that figure and compare it to a wage base of forty hours per week for fifty-two weeks, it's roughly $6.13 per hour and $245 per week.

The U.S. Department of Commerce statistics show that there are approximately thirteen million people on welfare. Based on a forty-hour work week, Welfare Recipients in thirty-nine states are given more than $8.00 per hour, in six states they are given more than

$12.00 per hour and in eight states they are given more than the average hourly wage of a teacher, Hawaii being the highest at $17.50 per hour. In addition to the welfare check, these individuals can also receive food stamps, housing and utility supplements and can still work and earn up to $1000.00 per month without a loss of benefits. If we take an average of just these welfare amounts across the United States it equals $12.50 per hour or $26,000 per year, not counting any other aid. Figuring thirteen million people on Welfare times $26,000.00 per year equals 338 Billion dollars just to support the welfare of thirteen million people. Welfare recipients receive more than two times as much pay before the additional aid as those who worked all their lives to support them and are now drawing social security benefits. I don't know about you, but to me that's just wrong.

There are no penalties for Welfare recipients who defraud the system. My second wife is a good example. I was in the Military and deployed to Okinawa Japan and she was pregnant. She was getting a check for all my pay except a small amount to pay for things I needed like personal hygiene items, laundry and haircuts. She could use the Base Hospital facilities while she was pregnant. She filed a claim for Welfare and because she was pregnant they also provided her a doctor and hospital care in the civilian community. None of which she needed. After the baby was born she left me and California and I was contacted to repay all the Welfare and hospital expenses. I informed the State Welfare Board the she had defrauded them based on the information above. They released me from the liability but never pursued her for the repayment.

Another problem with Social Security is the ability to defraud the system. There are no checks to keep a person from collecting on the Social Security account of a deceased person. What I mean is, if a person drawing Social Security dies but their bank account has another person on it with them, if the deceased isn't reported to Social Security the other person could draw the deceased person's Social Security for years. Likewise, if the deceased person had no heirs and was in a retirement or nursing facility and their checks were sent directly to the facility on behalf of that person, the facility could draw the Social Security for months before having to report the death and only then if the facility was to be audited or inspected by the state regulatory authority. There must be a means of insuring that Social Security Benefits are being paid to living persons or to the eligible descendants of those Social Security Beneficiaries.

What do you suppose was just added to the burden already

carried by Social Security? You guessed it, The Affordable Healthcare Act, Obamacare.

Have you figured out that we need to do something about our Government yet?

As late as the solution may be, since the Social Security Act has been broken for eighty years, there is still a solution.

1. Do not increase FICA and Medicare contributions. Leave them at 12.4%

2. Reduce Welfare payments to no more than the Federal Minimum Wage, **Period**. Make it less appealing to be on Welfare than to work. Cancel the Housing and Utility supplements. The Minimum Wage working people must make do with their wages to feed themselves, pay rent and utilities, **welfare can too.** If Churches want to provide these subsidies, let them, but take the burden off the tax payers.

3. Stop the additional money for having a lot of children. If a person has 15 kids, too bad, that Minimum Wage family from item #2 supports their family on their wages **welfare can too**. I believe that children need to be taken care of and would leave the Federal Aid for Dependent Children (FADC) and Women, Infants and Children (WIC) in place but do the math on what it costs monthly to feed and clothe a child.

4. Perform Random Drug testing on a percentage of Welfare recipients each month. If they are on drugs they no longer receive Welfare assistance.

5. Since the Social Security Act combined all the Welfare and Social Security into one place, leave it. This may sound like a contradiction, but the fact is we are paying 12.4% of our wages to FICA and Medicare. If we break out all the subjects individually it will cost us far more, because the working people will still be supporting those unable or unwilling to work and Government will tax us to provide that support.

6. Put the 2.4% part of the 12.4% contribution into an investment account for the Welfare Programs and let them work for the welfare recipients. Put the other 10% into a protected investment account for Social Security. For at least the first ten years these must be high yield accounts to try to make up the deficit in the current program. Don't

rely on surplus from a system that has no surplus available.

7. Make sure that the people who have worked and paid into the program receive more than those who haven't.

8. Take some of those under-employed IRS and other Government workers and send teams to the states to audit and investigate the welfare recipients and remove those that are fraudulently receiving benefits or misusing the benefits they receive. i.e. a person is drawing benefits for children that aren't living with them or the person is perfectly capable of working but chooses not to because they would rather sit at home and do nothing for the money. Audit those who spend vast amounts of their Welfare at casinos. They are obviously making too much if they can afford to throw it away gambling.

9. To prevent fraud in the Social Security System, tie the Social Security program to the IRS insomuch as if the IRS has a Social Security form 1099 but doesn't receive a tax return from that individual then the Social Security stops until the person reestablishes their existence and their right to the benefit.

10. Why are we Taxing Social Security? From its inception, it was a tax on our wages. FICA and Medicare are taxes on the net of a person's income, meaning that the money has already been taxed as income and then put into the Social Security System. Government is taxing us twice on the same dollar. STOP the taxation of Social Security Benefits. If Government feels a need to tax money derived from the Social Security Program, let them tax the Welfare recipients that make more than the Elderly who **need** Social Security to live. Tax welfare checks. As pointed out so far, I am not in favor of having an unconstitutional taxation of the individual but if we are going to have individual income tax then everyone needs to pay those taxes. We tax government employees and the military who receive their pay from the same taxes that pay welfare so why are we not taxing welfare, too.

There you have it, a solution to the Social Security and Welfare programs. If I stepped on a few toes, maybe you should re-evaluate your situation and become part of the solution instead of being part of the problem.

HEALTHCARE REFORM AND THE AFFORDABLE HEALTHCARE ACT (OBAMACARE)

"I predict future happiness for Americans if they can prevent the government from wasting the labors of the people under the pretense of taking care of them." - *Thomas Jefferson*

Since I'm talking about Taxes and since the Affordable Healthcare Act, Obamacare is a Tax regardless of claims by President Obama and Congress to the contrary, I felt that it should be addressed here.

Webster's Dictionary defines "Reform" as to make better or improve by removal of faults.

Does the United States need some type of Health Care Reform? Yes. Is the Affordable Healthcare Act (Obamacare) the answer? No. Obamacare is not a reform! It is a whole new program the tax payers of the United States are going to pay for in one way or another.

With health care and health insurance costs rising annually over the past several decades a reform plan is in order. Unfortunately, the solution isn't one which will be readily accepted by our Government. There is a very large and very tangled loop which is continually raising health care and insurance costs. This loop begins and ends with the Government. Government regulations require that Doctors and Hospitals are to maintain a certain amount of insurance against Malpractice. This type of insurance is called Professional Liability Insurance (PLI) and is common insurance for many professional service providers ranging from contractors to accountants to lawyers and doctors. There are very few legal suits brought against building contractors because of building code enforcement. The same is true of most of the businesses required by law to maintain PLI. Lawyers and Doctors however are continually under attack by family members and friends who feel their loved ones weren't given proper care or representation. Many of these lawyers and doctors incorporate themselves to protect their personal assets. Since I am talking specifically about Health Care Providers, I will get back to that subject. Because of being incorporated, most Doctors and Hospitals are also "For Profit" organizations, meaning that they make money, above their operating costs, for their services. They have shareholders and investors the hospital needs to ensure growth. This is business, and it will continue to be business if people need medical care. Here's where the loop starts. PLI is required by law passed by the government. Government also gave the public the right or power to present a legal suit against a person or business without regard to the degree of damages or perceived damages and with no Statute of Limitations. Here's a nationally known example of uncontrolled legal suits: A New Mexico resident ordered coffee from McDonald's Restaurant, commenced to place the coffee between his/her legs resulting in severe burns to their pelvic region. ABC news called the case "The poster child of excessive law suits."

Another, not so well known case is one that was presented and adjudicated in Linn County Iowa, where "Ineeda Roof" a fictitious plaintiff filed a real law suit against "Up on Top Roofing Company" a fictitious contractor and the Judge hearing the case ruled in favor of the plaintiff and awarded a considerable sum of money. Both cases were a waste of time and money, both by the parties involved and the tax payers, since we pay the judges.

Back to Health care. Obviously, Insurance companies provide PLI for the Doctors and Hospitals. When one of these entities is involved in a professional liability law suit, the insurance company provides legal support for the doctor or hospital involved and often settles the case before a lengthy trial that will cost much more in terms of money and time. When these cases are handled by the insurance provider, whether they are paid or not, the caregiver's insurance premiums go up. The Care Provider then must raise their service rates to make up the difference in the insurance premium. I'm not denying that health care providers don't make good money, they make very good money and live very good life styles, raises in their insurance affects them just as it does the rest of us. When hospital insurance premiums go up, so does the cost of hospitalization. People seeking medical care are hit with a double increase in medical care, first the doctors raise their fees, then the hospital raises theirs. The doctors and the hospital administrators, stockholders and investors are all happy because they can make more money even though a good portion of the money is going to the insurance company. I said that Government is the beginning and end of the Health Care loop. I've shown how Government is instrumental in rising Health Care costs by first requiring professionals to have PLI, then by allowing uncontrolled legal suits to be filed by the public. Well, Insurance is regulated by Government too. Insurance companies are only allowed to charge "x" number of dollars in premiums for certain types of insurance. They are also regulated in the number and types of claims they can payout. These regulations insure that the insurance companies will be able to support their customers and stay in business. When malpractice suits are filed against doctors and the PLI is reaching the limits of Government regulation, insurance companies appeal or lobby to Congress to raise the limitations so they can continue to provide adequate coverage for the doctors. Congress raises the limits and the whole process starts over again.

Solution: First, Government must decide upon a tort ruling to manage legal suits and give each type of suit a definitive maximum amount. This ruling must also make clear what types of cases may be filed and insure that the people filing the cases are real. This will reduce the number of cases frivolously brought against professionals.

Second, Government must regulate prices of goods and services, not only for the insurance companies but also for those professional services it requires to maintain PLI. I am not an advocate of more government control and regulation, but since the government is already regulating these professionals in part by the PLI requirement, then they should take an active interest in what services are provided and how much they should cost on a national average. If the national average, and I'm not talking big city average, cost of an emergency room visit is $50 then regulations should state that no hospital can charge more than the National average for that same care. Example, there are three cities in New Mexico, Santa Fe, Albuquerque and Socorro, with very divergent ethnic populations and demographics. These cities are no more than 100 miles apart. Medical costs between each of these cities are as divergent as their populations and the costs for like services even vary from hospital to hospital in the same community. (Regulate cost based on the services provided, then by the type of doctor seen for those services.) If I choose to go to my Heart Specialist to treat my cold, I should be expected to pay a little bit more, but if I go to an Urgent Care where

I'm seen by a Nurse Practitioner (NP), Physician's Assistant (PA) or an Intern, I should expect to pay less. In Albuquerque, New Mexico it costs more to be treated for a cold by the Hospital Urgent Care Physician's Assistant (PA) than it does to be treated by my Heart Specialist. After passing this regulation, pass the control and monitoring to the Groups that are already monitoring them. The American Medical Association, AMA, American Dental Association, ADA, the Bar Association for Lawyers, etc. There is no need for the government to then interfere with the routine operation of these groups, they must govern themselves. If there are issues or disputes within the groups, complaints can be made to a government agency like Health, Education, and Welfare, that already regulates them, to assist in resolving the issues. It doesn't ever reenter Congress. Once these regulations are passed, the pricing can be reviewed every other year by the monitoring group and any proposed change can be submitted to the regulating agency. No other deviation from the pricing is allowed, and any proposed bi-annual change must be approved by both houses of Congress.

This is Health Care Reform!

Here's the Patient Protection and Affordable Care Act (Obamacare) in a nutshell.

Obamacare was forced down the throats of the American people without regard to who is going to pay the final bill. Granted, Obamacare provides medical aid to those that need it but can't afford it. The problem with that thought is that someone must pay for that aid. If I need a heart procedure that costs $250,000 and I can't pay the bill, Obamacare will pay it for me not directly of course but through the mandated mandatory insurance. Where is Obamacare getting the money? From the tax payers! But **"this is not a tax."**

The insurance companies were relatively quick to jump on this money train, because they now have a permanent and indisputable income. Obamacare mandates that every American be insured and if they can't afford insurance they can purchase it through a Government co-operative. Who is the Co-operative? The insurance companies. How can they afford to sell insurance to the indigent for less than they sell it to the tax payers? Government subsidizes the difference. Who pays the subsidy? The Tax Payers! But **"this is not a tax."**

Doctors and Hospitals were also quick to jump on the money

train, because the "Affordable" in the act doesn't pertain to them. There is no reform to the way Medical professionals charge for their services and those services can continue to escalate at even greater speed than they did before, because the insurance companies are now required to pay the bill. The only thing that Obamacare makes "Affordable" is the cost of insurance to the indigent through the subsidies I mentioned above and We, The People are paying for them. But **this isn't a tax.** Not only are we paying for them, but we are paying for them twice, once through our taxes and the second time as our non-subsidized insurance premiums go up until we can no longer afford our own private insurance and must acquire our insurance through the government co-operative.

It has been historically proven that when a people become reliant upon the Government for their lives and livelihoods, they cannot or will not revolt against those in power for fear of losing what the Government gives them. The longer Obamacare stands, more and more people will become reliant on the Co-operative for their health care. I mentioned before that as businesses fail, and Obamacare is a catalyst, more and more people will join the ranks of welfare recipients. The writing is on the wall, many small businesses are already being forced to close because they cannot afford the insurance mandated by Obamacare. But, unemployment statistics are down. Why? Because those people who are losing their jobs feel hopeless and helpless to feed their families and keep their homes and are trading a possible paycheck for a guaranteed welfare check and aren't registering for unemployment.

Oh, and don't forget **"THIS IS NOT A TAX."** While we did not see a tax increase in 2012 or even in 2013, what we did see was higher limits on medical deduction before they can be claimed and loss of some other deductions that we used to be able to claim. Before Obamacare, 2012 and earlier tax years, the standard deduction for Medical was 7% of your adjusted gross income. After Obamacare, 2013, that standard deduction for Medical was raised to 10% of your adjusted gross income. Even though there was no "Official Tax Increase", taxes were increased because the deduction was raised limiting the number of people that could claim it. This increase in the eligible deduction amount significantly raised the taxes of those persons that have minimal medical bills. In 2013 the ability to claim Medical Insurance as part of the Standard Medical Deduction was also significantly reduced. Yes, the Government didn't raise the amount of taxes we are required to pay, but by changing the deductions we could claim to reduce our tax burden, they have hidden the fact that our taxes went up to cover Obamacare. For the 2014 tax year, saw some major problems. First, if you didn't have proof of your insurance coverage you wouldn't see a Tax refund even though you had one due to you. Second, if you didn't have proof of insurance you had to pay a penalty of up to 5% of your taxes unless you were otherwise exempt. But who was exempt? If you were incarcerated for as much as a single day during 2014, you are exempt from the penalty. If you were on Welfare during any time in 2014 you are exempt. If you are in the country illegally, you are exempt. Where are the exemptions for the hard-working Americans that are supporting this program? There aren't any! But remember **"THIS IS NOT A TAX!"** And remember the Unconstitutional 16th Amendment gave them the ability to do this.

On the lighter side. Another email circulating on the internet reads "Obamacare Deciphered." This email although humorous gives a fair analogy of the legalese and rhetoric of the affordable healthcare act, condensing the ten thousand plus pages to four sentences. This isn't quite true but close.

1. To begin: To insure the uninsured, we first must un-insure, those who are insured.

2. Next, we require the newly uninsured, to be re-insured.

3. Then, to re-insure those previously insured, who are now the newly uninsured, they must pay a penalty charge to be re-insured.

4. And finally, this extra charge is by necessity so that those originally insured, who became the newly uninsured, and then had to be re-insured, will pay enough extra to cover the cost of insuring the originally uninsured so that they can now be insured, at no cost to themselves. Since originally publishing this book in 2015. Several of the major insurance companies have opted out of Obamacare. Why? Because they are losing money and cannot continue to pay the insurance claims and keep their doors open. We, the people cannot opt out of the program but the people we must get our insurance from can. The pool of companies that provide the mandatory Obamacare insurance is getting smaller and soon won't exist leaving us to have to join the state health co-ops which are in no way cheap. We seriously need to repeal Obamacare.

EDUCATION

For years, we have been troubled by the poor level of education in this Country. There have been proposals to only give pay increases to teachers, based on the number of children passed to the next grade. This idea is possibly the most idiotic of all the proposed methods to raise the level of education. Delaying any type of pay for teachers on this basis only defeats the purpose. They will summarily pass all their students regardless of ability so they will get their pay increases.

There have been tests developed to measure a child's academic ability and standing among their age and grade peers on the National level. This is also a stupid idea. Most of these tests have been forced down the throats of State Educators by the same Congress that lines its pockets with money from PACs. The fact here is these tests are not the product of educators. They are a product of the companies that supply the test materials so they can make more money and profit. They contribute to PACs and influence our Congress to implement the tests on a National basis. The cheapest of these was probably the Iowa Assessment Test. Imagine the amount of money to be made on that test since it was once in **every** school in the United States. Now Comes the Partnership for Assessment of Readiness for College and Careers test (PARCC) test. The PARCC is given online to grades 3-11. You cannot tell me that the big computer and computer software industry did not have anything to do with this test. Every school that accepts the PARCC program must buy enough computers, software and teacher and administrator training to give the test to hundreds of thousands of students and it is not just an assessment of high school students getting ready to enter college or career fields. It spans all schools; elementary schools, middle schools, Junior high schools and high schools. Who gets the benefit? The computer technology industry, specifically the programs biggest supporter - Microsoft.

Children are not test scores! There have been numerous studies and great amounts of research since the 1950s concerning the national testing of students. Researchers have determined that twenty-five to forty percent of all students suffer from test anxiety and these students score on average twelve to twenty percentile points below their peers. Forty percent of any test group severely skews the result. What do these tests measure? Absolutely **NOTHING!** They do not measure the child's ability to learn nor do they measure the ability of the teacher to teach. They do not measure all the students equally for their ability to learn or retain the information. All the tests accomplish is to put undue stress on the children. If the teacher has not taught the student to read or the parents have not encouraged their child to learn – how are they supposed to pass a test?

You cannot expect the average child from the ghetto or projects schools to achieve the same score as the average child from an upper middle class school or even the average child from the affluent upper class or private schools. It is not that the teaching or curriculum is any different. It's the prevailing under tone in each of these communities that dictates how well a child learns. Distractions from the street, peer pressure and the community influence a child's ability to learn and a teacher's ability to teach that child.

Children are measured and evaluated every day based on their performance of the work presented in their classrooms. That should be sufficient to determine their ability to learn. Teachers are paid to educate, measure and evaluate our children. If a student is failing – it is the teacher's job to provide that student with the tools to succeed. Those tools can be, but are not limited to:

Talk to the student –

Is there something in the information they do not understand?

Is there anything going on at home that may be an issue? Divorce? Death?

Are there troubles with their peers that may be an issue?

Talk to parents, same questions as above, and not just at PTA meetings

Talk to other teachers, do they know anything about the child?

Provide additional assistance (possibly after school hours).

Pair them with a more proficient student as a tutor.

It is ludicrous to continue testing our children to measure the performance of their teachers. In 2014, New Mexico began an online testing of students, the PARCC. Another test that replaces the existing assessment test? This test was developed by a coalition of states for evaluating children in grades 3-11. **What?** Did anyone look at the title of this test? **Assessment of Readiness for College and Careers**. What are we doing giving this test to elementary school students, grade 3-6? I do not think my eight-year-old grandchildren are quite ready to enter college or the work place, unless of course our Government has also changed the child labor laws. Which, I would not doubt they have done or at least tried. I understand the test is different for students in each grade level but whoever thought up the name needs some serious help. New Jersey was the initial test bed for the PARCC. It was inconclusive and deemed a failure. In other states the test failed to achieve desired results. A couple of the States wanted to withdraw from the program but were not allowed to by the Federal Government. As the results have proven the test to be a failure, two of the original four tests have been removed from the basic test and revised and added as optional tests. When the PARCC was presented in New Mexico, students in many of the state's High Schools walked out of their classes in protest. One group of students, with the assistance of their media teacher, produced a video that was posted on YouTube. **"I am NOT a test score"**

As I said, our children are measured and evaluated every day of their academic lives. If we need to evaluate the teachers, don't test the children to do it. Instead survey the children with twenty-five essay type questions, given after having had the teacher for a minimum of three months. Our children are amazing! If given the opportunity to raise the standard of their education – most will jump on that opportunity. Our children want to learn and they recognize good and bad teachers by whether they feel they are learning from them. Many of us can remember those teachers that were particularly bad and good from our school days. At sixty-four years old, I can still remember my second-grade teacher, an aged hag with nothing but a scowl and disdain for her students. I also remember my third-grade teacher, a woman with a pleasant smile and sincere devotion to her students, who reinforced that learning can be fun and to that end I have continued to pursue learning throughout my life. Listen to the children! They will give us a far better evaluation of our teachers and educational processes and problems than any myriad of tests.

If we need more evaluation of our teachers, survey the parents of the students. Parents also know the good and bad teachers based on talks with their children and the amount of time spent working with their children to help them understand the subjects.

I mentioned in the opening paragraphs of this chapter that through the PAC our Congress is influenced to establish these "educational" evaluation tools. What does Congress do with them? They create Doctrines like the "No Child Left Behind" (NCLB) program, which by the name alone indicates the state educators will pass the children along so they stay with their peer group. The Child will not be held back even though they may not be ready to advance. The NCLB was not really directed to pass every child regardless of ability. It was directed at the teachers and their ability to keep the children educated to the same level – Left behind the level of their peers nationally.

Congress wanted this program established throughout the country, so they gave the states an incentive to participate. The States that participated would receive extra money for education, those States that did not want to participate would have a reduction in Federal Education funding. Congress was bribing the States to conform to its will for the NCLB program. **The NCLB is a failure!**

The latest of these programs is the "Race to the Top" (RTTT) program which rewards schools and State Departments of Education for improving the education level of the school system. Again, Congress has bribed the States to conform. They want every state to participate in the program, they reward those states that accept the program and withhold funds from those that do not accept the program.

The singular item that makes these programs even worse is they were mandated to the states while the state congress was in recess or during the summer break from school. The deadlines for answering were before the State Congress was to reconvene. Many states were not able to submit the acceptance through their Congress for approval or comment. Either the Governor or the State Board of Education had to make the decision for the State which is against the bylaws of most State Constitutions and violates Federal Statutes concerning education.

We cannot use a shotgun approach to raising the education level of the country. All the programs Government has established have addressed the problem, but have avoided the answer. To fix the problem, you need to evaluate each subject involved in creating the problem and determine the best way to solve the problems one at a time instead of trying to fix them all with one program.

<u>Testing is NOT the Answer!</u>
<u>Programs like NCLB and RTTT are NOT the answer either!</u>

THE FEDERAL RESERVE ACT, THE "FED"

Because of the drafting and proposal of the 16th Amendment, 1909 was not a very good year for the American people. The four years that followed weren't much better - all culminating in 1913, the worst year for the American people outside of the war years.

To explain this section, it is important to understand a couple of things about our Government. First, William Taft (R) was President in 1910 and in the House, the Republican Party was in the majority. The election of 1912 transferred the House majority to the Democrats and Woodrow Wilson (D) was elected to the Presidency and was sworn into office March 4th 1913. Secondly, we cannot place blame for our current situation on either party, Republican or Democrat, without casting that blame on the party system. Because of the Party System our Representatives fear they must follow the party line or risk having the party exempt them from the next election thereby prematurely ending their careers. Thus, Democrats, will not vote for Republican bills and vice versa without adding the opposing parties view and the Tea Party and Independent Parties would not vote with any other party without adding their two cents into the mix as well. **What happened to the People's view?**

In 1910, The United States needed a reform of the banking structure to stabilize the economy. The big banks in New York, called the banking trust that I mentioned earlier, commanded a great deal of control over the banking industry. The public demand was to break the banking trust. Under a cloak of secrecy, Senator Nelson Aldrich (R) (remember him from the chapter on the 16th amendment) and five other men, who were later identified as the leading big bankers of the period, traveled to a remote island off the coast of Georgia, Jekyll Island. During the late 1800s and early 1900s, Jekyll

Island was a resort, privately owned by members of the country's elite upper class. I am not going to get into all the details of who was in the Jekyll Island Group. If you want those details, you can research them yourself and/or read the book "The Creature from Jekyll Island" by G. Edward Griffin.

The fact is, in 1910, these five members of the country's financial elite and the Senator charged with safekeeping the Nation's finances, secretly sat on Jekyll Island for nine days and drafted the plan for the Federal Reserve System. Normally, there would be no need for secrecy. Bankers regularly got together in various meetings and frequently traveled to Jekyll Island on vacation trips. The secrecy was dictated by the fact that this time a prominent Senator and Chairman of the National Finance Committee was at the meeting. Think about that for a minute, 5 bankers and the Manager of the Nation's Finances, planning the future of the American Banking System.

It should be noted here that Senator Aldrich was also tied strongly to the Rockefeller family, since his daughter was married to John D. Rockefeller Jr. Remember that the Rockefeller's were part of the banking trust that came out of the country's westward movement.

Here on Jekyll Island, we have basically 6 representatives of the banking community planning and deciding the fate of the nation's financial security. As Griffin puts it "we have allowed the fox to build the hen house and install the security system".

The Jekyll Island meeting accomplished two very significant changes to American banking. The first change united the bankers. Until this point these bankers had been in competition with each other, vying for supremacy over the banking trust. Not being able to gain supremacy, or to drive their competitors out of the market, the bankers agreed to work together for a common interest -- that interest being to control all the money in the United States. These bankers formed a Cartel. Now here's a word we generally hear associated with South American Drug Lords, but Webster's Dictionary defines a cartel as *"a combination of independent business enterprises designed to limit competition". Synonyms for Cartel are Monopoly and Syndicate.* Now in 1910 we have a banking Cartel, made up of the biggest and strongest banks in the country, writing a bill that will ultimately give them control over all the nation's money.

I will talk about the second change in a minute. For simplicity, I will refer to this cartel as Big Bank.

After the meeting on Jekyll Island, Senator Aldrich presented the Aldrich Bill to the Democratic Controlled Congress. This Bill outlined the Federal Reserve System as it had been devised by the group of bankers. The Bill was defeated. This defeat may have been because of Aldrich's ties to the Rockefeller family and banking or because there were some bad feelings about the way Aldrich handled the 16th Amendment proposal or possibly because in its original form it too closely resembled the Central Bank of England which the 1910 Congress recognized as having problems stabilizing England's economy. At any length and for any number of reasons the bill was not passed.

In 1912, as stated earlier, the Democrats gained control of the House. The wording, but not the intent, of the Aldrich Bill was rearranged, Aldrich's name was removed so it became the Federal Reserve Act and some restrictions were added. The restrictions limited the "Feds" influence over the nation's money and the "new" bill gave a kind of lending institution to Congress allowing them to draw advances on a small percentage of uncollected taxes and required these advances to be paid back after taxes were collected. In December, 1913, the "new" Federal Reserve Act was presented to the House. This time it passed and was signed into law on December 23, 1913 by President Woodrow Wilson (D)

December 23rd is a rather important date for Government. Two days before Christmas, most of our representatives, both then and now, are more concerned with getting home to their families for the holiday than they are in reading through many pages of text in a bill. They look briefly at the summary and vote; thus, it is more likely for a bill to be passed on this day than on any other day of the year.

The second change was that The Federal Reserve Act formed a kind of partnership between the bankers and the government. Through the Federal Reserve System, Government could get an advance on a small percentage of uncollected taxes. Congress thought this was a great idea, because it could continue operating and funding new programs or appropriations without having to worry about having the money in the Treasury. This was good for the country, it kept our Government working in lean times of the year.

What made this partnership hazardous to the American people, was the amendment to the Federal Reserve Act that was passed in 1914. In 1914, amendments were passed to the Federal Reserve Act removing all the restrictive wording and protections that were included in the original Act and gave our government the right to abuse their trust and power in direct violation of the Constitution and the Bill of Rights. This amendment removed the restrictions that limited the Fed's control and Congress could draw unlimited funds from the "Fed" and no longer had a requirement to pay back the advances. The bankers had convinced Congress that the restrictions weren't necessary, because the Fed was set up with a Presidential Nominee as the Head of the Federal Reserve. Paying back the advances would be tantamount to double taxing the public, since both the advance and the repayment would be coming from the public taxes. This opened the door for these advances to grow into a blatant misuse of Public funds.

All the banking transactions throughout the United States are processed through the Federal Reserve System. The sheer volume of business this creates would require a huge number of staff and real estate if performed by one facility. By dividing up the country into banking districts the burden becomes less on the central facility. Federal Reserve Banks aren't banks at all, they were given the title Bank in the Federal Reserve Act to give Small Bank a place to hold their reserve. Today these are broken down even further into branches of the Federal Reserve Bank. There are twelve Federal Reserve Banks, one for each of the Federal Districts Established by the Federal Reserve Act of 1913. There are twenty-four Branch Banks to the Federal Reserve Banks, but not every Federal Reserve Bank has Branches. Each Federal Reserve Bank and Branch has the responsibility to maintain control of the banking activity in their respective district or area.

This gives you a brief history of the origins and operation of the Federal Reserve System, so let's look at what this system is or isn't:

Number 1: The Federal Reserve System is not a Federal entity. It is not controlled by the government, nor does it have to answer to the government. It is a private Corporation and who do you think is on the Board of this corporation? Big Bank. The Head of the Federal Reserve is a person Appointed by the President, but that person is just a figurehead, a show piece to give the impression that the Federal Reserve is part of the Government. They have no real input into the workings of the Fed. The Board (Big Bank) controls the Fed.

Number 2: The Federal Reserve System itself does not hold any money or Reserves. The Federal Reserve Banks hold reserves and pay interest to the individual (Small Bank) banks for those reserved Funds, but that is a story of its own.

Number 3: The Federal Reserve System is not a System at all. As stated in Number 1, it is a private corporation that regulates all things monetary in the United States.

Number 4: The Federal Reserve System was formed to stabilize the U.S. economy and has failed miserably in that mission. The great depression (1929-1939) began a mere sixteen years after the signing of the Federal Reserve Act and should have been the greatest reinforcement that the Fed could not do the job for which it was commissioned. The roller coaster ride the economy has been on for the last century should further attest to the fact that the Federal Reserve System is a failure and should be abolished. Furthermore, the U.S. Dollar has lost 90 percent of its value since the beginning of the Federal Reserve.

Number 5: The Federal Reserve Building and the thirty-six Federal Reserve Banks were paid for and built with tax payer dollars. The Federal Government spent tax money to build facilities for a private corporation without the people's knowledge or approval.

Looking at these five things, it becomes clear that the bankers who met on Jekyll Island accomplished their prime objective -- Gaining control of all the money in the United States.

Until the passage of the Federal Reserve Act, banks could only lend money based upon the amount of money secured by depositors. Simply put if the bank had $100 deposited, they could loan $100. After the Federal Reserve Act was passed, the Fed allowed, and still allows, the same bank with the same $100 deposited to loan up to $900. Where does the extra $800 come from? The Fed requires Small bank to place 10% of every deposit in Reserve. This is where item number 2 comes into play. Here's how it breaks down:

$100 is deposited into an account in a local bank, Small Bank. Small Bank deposits the required 10% or $10 into the Federal Reserve Bank, and Loans John Smith $90. Let's say Small Bank charges 10% or $9 interest (called a discount) on the loan. John Smith must pay Small Bank $99 to pay off the loan. The Federal Reserve Bank then pays a rediscounted amount for John Smith's loan to keep Small Bank solvent. This rediscounted amount will be about $94.50, the amount loaned to John Smith plus one half of the interest. Basically, buying the note from Small Bank. Now Small Bank has $94.50. Since this rediscount is considered a deposit, Small Bank is now required to deposit 10% into the Federal Reserve Bank and will have $85.05 they can loan to Mary Jones and the cycle starts over again. This is where the additional $800 comes from. By this method of accounting, Small Bank can loan the same $100 approximately 70 times.

On the surface this all looks promising. The Federal Reserve Bank immediately pays back whatever money Small Bank has made in loans with partial interest. Small Banks now has more money available for loans to people who want them. And the Fed pays interest on the reserve money Small Bank has deposited.

Here's the catch;

1) The interest the Federal Reserve Bank pays to Small Bank is about 6%. The interest Small Bank pays on your Savings is less than one half of 1%. What is Small Bank doing with the other 5.5%?

2) The money the Federal Reserve Banks has on deposit or in reserve from Small Bank is there to keep the Small Bank from going out of business. The interest paid on the reserve is to encourage growth of the bank – more branches with more depositors and more loans. The Question is: Where is the money coming from that the Federal Reserve Bank uses to pay interest to Small Bank?

3) Once Small Bank has made loans of $900 on the $100 they had on deposit, The Federal Reserve Bank only has the $100 from Small Bank in reserve. Where did the Federal Reserve Bank get the money to pay the rediscounts to Small Bank for the money they lent out?

4) The Federal Reserve Banks are not lending institutions or banks at all. You can't walk into one and open an account, take out a loan or make a loan payment. They don't invest Small Bank's money to make more money for the interest payments. They exist solely for keeping the doors open at Small Bank, the interest money on Small Banks Reserve isn't coming from the interest paid on the Small Bank loan. You will see where this money is coming from in a minute.

What's happening to the payments that John Smith is making? Big Bank basically buys the note again from the Federal Reserve Bank for $95. The Fed uses this money to pay the interest on Small Banks Reserve. John Smith thinks he's paying Small Bank, but they already have the repayment of his loan from the Federal Reserve Bank. John is going to pay the full $99 to Big Bank without his knowledge and Big Bank is going to make a nice profit of $4, which they didn't work for. Multiply this $4 by all the loans generated each day and it becomes quite apparent how Big Bank stays in control over the monetary affairs of the Country. The Federal Reserve System controls not only the Federal Reserve Banks but all banks. The Fed can dictate the number of branches each bank has, who the branch managers are and who the bank president is. It controls interest rates on loans and savings as well as dividends paid to stockholders. Yes, Big Bank accomplished their goal: **They have control of everything monetary in the country.**

Consider this: if an average home costs $100,000.00 and 70 homes are purchased, the total loan amount from the bank would be $7,000,000. At prime interest, it will cost the buyer approximately $272,000, if repaid over a standard 30-year term, that's $100,000 in principle and $172.000 in interest. Now multiply that times 70 (the number of times a bank can loan the same money), $12,040,000 in interest alone and what did the bank have to keep in reserve to be able to secure these 70 loans. Only the 10% or $700,000. Since these loans have been rediscounted by the Federal Reserve Bank and Big Bank has paid the Federal Reserve Bank that means Big Bank instantly realizes a gain of 6.3 million dollars, then makes over 11 million dollars profit from interest over the term of those home loans. In addition to this basic interest many banks collect the Principle, Interest, Tax (Property taxes) and Insurance (PITI) on these home mortgages. Principle and Interest are what is paying off the mortgage, but the Tax and Insurance are not. Property taxes are normally collected two times a year usually May and October. The Bank that collects Taxes as part of the payment divides the projected annual property tax over twelve months and collects a monthly payment. This monthly payment sits in an account drawing interest for six months until the first installment of property tax is due to the County. Where does the interest go? Into the pockets of the bank. The bank will declare that this interest pays for the servicing of the tax payment, but consider all the mortgages carried by the bank and the amount of interest they collect, that's a lot of money just for servicing the property taxes. Insurance is even worse because most home owner's insurance is paid annually, the money collected by the bank draws a full year's interest before being used for the insurance payment.

Here's the other side of the Federal Reserve System, if the Congress needs a billion dollars for some program and the treasury doesn't have the money, they go to the "Fed" who writes the check. The "Fed" needs to pay the interest on Small Banks Reserve, it goes back to the treasury and says we need more money printed so we can continue to support Small Bank, the public and the government. The treasury asks the House of Representatives for permission to print more money for the Fed to support the people. In the interest of helping the people the House approves the measure and the Treasury then prints more money in the form of Federal Reserve Notes, without collateral backing, causing inflation to rise, because the more paper that is on the street -- the less it's worth. Paper currency must have some type of backing, normally gold or silver or some other precious material. Since there is only so much gold available the "Fed" has just created money from thin air reducing the value of the dollar.

When inflation rises, the price of commodities go up along with the cost of doing business. Small business cannot compete with the larger ones, because their incomes won't support the higher cost of goods and materials, the business goes under. When the small businesses close, unemployment goes up. Unemployment creates two major situations.

(1) The number of people on social welfare goes up because people need a way to feed their families.

(2) Those who were employed and had assets tied up as collateral for loans, lose those assets since they can no longer pay the debt.

There is a 3rd situation that rises from unemployment and that is false labor statistics. The longer people are on welfare the less likely they are to look for gainful employment. At the beginning of a recession labor statistics show many unemployed because people who have worked are looking for work. As unemployment benefits run out, after about eighteen months in most states, these unemployed workers start to fall off the State unemployment rolls and more and more join the welfare rolls. Also, people who are minimum retirement age of 62 years old do not count in labor statistics as unemployed even though they may still want to work until age 66 or 70 to get their full Social Security.

Back to lost collateral, who gets those assets held as collateral? Small Bank holds the collateral because they are local. Big Bank doesn't want to get tied up in the collateral if the note should default. What does Small Bank do with them? Small Bank repossesses and resells them for less than their value to a person who is still employed and can take out a new loan. They pay off the debt note held by Big Bank and put their 10% of the remainder of the proceeds into the Reserve Bank and Loan out the rest, starting the whole cycle over again and creating more interest for the Big Bank.

Remember John Smith that took out the $99 loan? Let's take a closer look at Mr. Smith's account:

John used his car as collateral for the loan. The car was only worth about $150 but since the value was more than the loan, Small Bank issued the note.

John pays on the loan for 4 months, we'll say $40 total, and loses his job and is no longer able to repay the loan.

Small Bank repossesses John's car and sells it for $55, the balance owing to Big Bank for paying off the Fed. Big Bank is happy, they didn't lose anything except the interest and they will make that up on the next loan.

John still owes $4 of the original loan, called the residual. He's unemployed and cannot pay the residual. Small Bank files a collection against John and his credit is trashed, he can't borrow any more money from anyone or get a credit card.

John has used up his 18 months of unemployment so to feed his family he applies to welfare.

John now makes as much or more, because of food stamps, housing supplements, utility supplements and the welfare check, than he did when he was working. Why would John return to the grind of getting up every morning to beat himself up for a paycheck, when he can sit at home and do nothing for the same money or better. What caused John's plight? John was employed by small business. Inflation caused small business to cut back employees and eventually go out of business. John was a median skilled worker, like most in the country, therefore, employment opportunities were limited and paid generally less than he gained on welfare.

I have discussed Welfare in the chapter on Social Security.

I know there have been many books, magazine articles and news reports on the Fed including the Griffin book I mentioned on page 86 and many people are skeptical about their validity. Everyone knows that something must be done about the Fed.

Government's solution is to audit the Fed. An Audit will waste time and only prove that the Fed is doing exactly what it says its doing and the bookkeeping will be found to be in perfect order. The problem with trying to describe the Fed and how it works is that you must dig through about 10,000 pages of minutia and legalese to get down to the basic make up and purpose of the Fed. The fact is the Fed needs to be abolished. It was supposed to stabilize the economy. It hasn't! In fact, it has created a greater economic problem. If every bank in the United States is supposed to be depositing 10% of each depositors account in the Federal Reserve Bank for the last 100 years, considering the number of accounts that have been opened over that period and the number of banks receiving deposits, why are there only a little over 3 trillion dollars in the Federal Reserve Banks. Now the Fed is supposed to have enough money to bail out Small Bank if they are having problems. They don't! Well maybe - just enough to help a few banks, but nowhere near enough to prevent a major bank run on a lot of banks at the same time. If Big Bank had a run on the bank at the same time hundreds of Small Banks were experiencing runs, the Fed would bail out the Big Banks and many of the Small Banks would fail. Sorry Boys, there just is not enough to go around. That's basically what happened in the crash of 2008. The Fed did not have the money to support a bail out of all the banks. The Government had to borrow money from other countries, particularly China to fill the gap. Where did the money go? It went to our government. It went to Big Bank. And it now supports the IMF, the International Monetary Fund which supports third world countries. But it's not where it's supposed to be - in the Reserve Bank helping to stabilize our economy and being a reserve to keep banks in business. This lack of funds in the Reserve Bank became apparent when the government had to use tax dollars and borrowed money from other countries to bail out AIG and Citibank in the mid-2000s. This is your money. Money that is supposed to be protecting your bank from going broke.

If you have any doubt about Big Bank and Government being in bed together, look at the Big Bank history and Bailouts of 2008. The Big Banks in the United States are Citibank, Bank of America, J P Morgan Chase and Wells Fargo. These form the bulk of the Big Bank Cartel members

Citigroup or Citi is an American multinational bank and financial services corporation headquartered in Manhattan, NY. In 1998 Citi merged with Travelers Group (a financial conglomerate) in one of the largest mergers in history making it the third largest bank holding company in the U.S. by the beginning of 2008. Its largest shareholders were from the Middle East and Singapore, China. In 2007, Citi was one of the primary dealers in U.S. Treasury Securities. Meaning they buy Securities directly from the Treasury and resell them to others. By the Global Financial Crisis of 2008, Citi was the largest company and bank in the world in total assets, holding over 200 million customer accounts in 140 different countries. Citi supposedly suffered great loses in the Crisis of 2008 and in November of 2008 our Government rescued them with a massive stimulus package. The Government took a 36% equity stake in Citi meaning that 36% of the Stock of the company was given to our Government as collateral for the package. Not a bad deal on the surface. Here's what the package entailed: $25 billion in emergency aid, a $45 billion line of credit to prevent bankruptcy, a guarantee against loss on troubled assets of $300 billion and an immediate $20 billion injection into the company. The package was initially worth $390 million, a tidy little sum given to Citi which held the largest number of assets in the world. There were some restrictions to the salaries of Citi's CEO and Executives, the CEO could only receive a salary of $1 per year and the executive salaries could not exceed $500,000 per year. Any portion of their salary that exceeded these amounts was paid in restricted stock. Now this restricted stock is stock that cannot be sold until certain conditions are met within the company. In this case the debt to the government had to be fully repaid. The Government also gained control of half the seats on Citi's Board of Directors. Who filled these seats and how was their selection decided? These seats were filled by appointment by the President of the United States, specifically President Obama. I could find no documentation on who filled the seats. Government also had the responsibility of removing any of Citi's Senior Management if there were indications of poor performance. Here's a case of the "pot calling the kettle black". We have a Government that performs poorly on an epidemic scale determining the poor performance of Citigroup's management which had built one of the largest corporations in the world.

In 2009, Citi sold $21 billion of its shares and by 2010 Citi had paid the $45 billion Line of Credit in full. Our Government sold 9% of its shares and in December sold the remaining 27% of their stock for a combined profit of just over $12 billion. Government says the Citi bank paid their debt in full. Let's do the math. Government received $12 billion profit on the sale of the stock. Citi Paid the Emergency Aid of $25 billion, and the $45 Billion Line of Credit. We don't know how much of the $300 billion guarantee was used. Citi owed another $20 billion for the immediate injection. Citi, as far as we can tell from the documents available, paid $82 billion of a $390 billion debt. If these repayment figures are correct, Citi still owes the Government approximately $308 billion more. Why hasn't Citi paid back the $308 billion it still owes the Government?

The other thing that Government did in this case that reflects their partnership with Big Bank, they exempted Citi from having to pay taxes until their debt was paid. In my opinion Citi now owes the back taxes for the three years of tax exemption, plus interest and fees.

As of 2012, Citi had built up a huge cash reserve of over $420 billion in liquid surplus cash by selling off the troubled assets the Treasury had guaranteed for $300 billion for $500 billion.

In 2008 while Citi was struggling against losses from the Global Financial Crisis, the Fed, was providing funds and guarantees to J P Morgan Chase Bank to enable them to purchase Bear Stern's Companies. Bear Stearns was a large financial institution with substantial mortgage backed securities. Since Chase was the largest and most financially solvent bank in the U. S. and was not affected by the crisis, why was the Fed helping them purchase Bear Stearns?

Here's another example of where our Government is in bed with big bank. Since 1919, AIG has had a brutal history of corruption, graft and pandering with the IRS, Securities and Exchange Commission and Department of Justice as well as several State Governments. On several these occasions, they have been found guilty and liable for their actions and had to repay investors and account holders billions of dollars. Yet in 2007 and 2008 the Fed and our government provided $182.3 billion to keep AIG afloat. The agreement gave Government a 79.9% equity stake in the AIG. It was not until AIG boasted that they were paying their executives and CEO bonuses exceeding $165 million and total bonuses could reach $450 million after reporting a net loss that the Government became outraged and moved to block the bonuses. Since 2008, AIG has sold most of its assets and holdings to pay back the government loan, The Government has sold its AIG Stock, and in January 2009, the Board of AIG discussed a lawsuit against the Government claiming the bailout they received was unfair to their investors. The idea was rejected.

When the Savings and Loan Scandal happened, the Government closed them and prosecuted the owners and board members. Why is AIG allowed to remain in business? Ladies and Gentlemen, if you have investments or accounts with AIG, it would be a good idea to rethink them and soon. Hopefully, in the next financial crisis AIG will not see the same amount of support from the Government. How does AIG stay in business? It is a member of the Big Bank cartel. If you don't believe it, consider this, in September 2014, AIG appointed Peter Hancock (does the name sound familiar?) as their new CEO. Mr. Hancock had a twenty-year history with J.P. Morgan Chase.

How do we break the power hold? This is a question of some magnitude, since Big Bank and Government are allied to each other, well entrenched and determined to hold onto the Fed.

Here's the solution: Big Bank relies on the interest from credit to maintain their cash flow and that cash flow equates to their power. It stands to reason that if the people and industry would stop assuming more and more credit debt, we would eventually stop the river of money going into the pockets of Big Bank.

To show how this would work we need to visit The Central Bank of Europe. In the summer of 2014, the Small Banks of Europe weren't issuing enough loans to satisfy Big Bank Europe's greed, they adjusted the Central Bank of Europe's interest rate on reserve deposits to negative 1%. What this meant was, that Small Bank Europe, who was getting 6 to 6.5 percent on their deposits now had to pay to place their money in reserve in the Central Bank. Central Bank had reduced interest rates to encourage more people to take out loans and establish credit. It didn't work. The European people and industry feared another major recession and wanted their finances to survive without the added burden of credit debt. If the people continue to avoid credit debt, Small Bank Europe will lose money because of the negative interest, thus causing them to fail. Once the small banks begin to fail, the larger banks will begin to fail and the Central bank system will fail because they do not have the funds available to keep every bank in Europe stable. Without the cash flow from interest, Big Bank Europe will lose its power hold over Europe, because the Government must develop a new and better system to stabilize their economy. In the United States, we have the same problem. Since Big Bank holds all our notes, they control the flow of money and power. People aren't taking on as much credit debt and the Fed has been reducing interest rates for years. If we all stop creating credit debt, then the Fed must start charging interest on Small Bank's Reserve causing Small Bank to fail, then the Fed will fail. A huge key and major factor is that we must be ready when Small Bank begins to fail. If we have large amounts of our money tied up in Small Bank and the Stock Market when Small Bank goes down, we could have another great depression and people will suffer. We cannot have large amounts of money tied up in the stock market or in banks. The Fed must protect Small Bank against a run on the bank and bail them out where possible. But the Fed only has so much money and the Treasury cannot print the kind of money that will help save all the banks and the Fed. As it was during the Great Depression, your bank probably won't have the money to support a run on the bank and like the Great Depression the only survivors will be Big Bank and Big

Industry.

Even if the President was inclined to issue an Executive Order to abolish the Fed, unless there is a system to replace the Fed, the order would be disastrous. All banking and the stock markets are tied together. In the United States the bond is the Fed. In Europe, it's tied to the Central Bank and the Eastern Countries have their own version for these two banking entities. These entities are tied together by Big Bank. If an order was issued to immediately dissolve the Fed, all banking would instantly fail. There would be no longer be a system for the conveyance of funds from one location to another except through the regular postal service. The lack of speed would cause the banking industry to virtually grind to a halt. Small Bank would go first because they don't have the assets to sustain them. The stock market would suffer next because trade transactions wouldn't be able to transfer money for purchases or sales fast enough, causing a panic among the serious and heavily invested. Without Small Bank and the Stock market, Big Bank would also fail. Our currency would devalue completely and the world markets would start to collapse. This isn't a scare tactic like you see on the Internet or junk mail to get you to purchase gold or some other folly, it is a fact. If you purchased this book, it wasn't because I gave you a forty-minute spiel of doom to persuade you to buy it.

We can't expect our Government to help us very much since our elected officials use the Big Bank and Big Industry to fund campaigns. It would not be in their best interest to vote against the special interests of these benefactors and contributors. Before we crash the Fed, We, The People, need to get control of our elected officials. **This Solution is coming, possibly sooner than you might think.**

"As a very important source of strength and security, cherish public credit. One method of preserving it is, to use it as sparingly as possible; avoiding occasions of expense by cultivating peace, but remembering also that timely disbursements to prepare for danger frequently prevent much greater disbursements to repel it; avoiding likewise the accumulation of debt, not only by shunning occasions of expense, but by vigorous exertions in time of peace to discharge the debts, which unavoidable wars may have occasioned, not ungenerously throwing upon posterity the burden, which we ourselves ought to bear." – George Washington

THE PRESIDENT AND VICE PRESIDENT

When I first started thinking about this chapter, I felt that the president and vice president should not be combined (by Party) in any election, that the Candidates should run as individuals. The winner of the election would become the president and the candidate with the next higher vote would become the vice president. It is unlikely that Congress would sit divided on issues because of party affiliation since if anything happened to the President the Vice-President a member of the opposing party would then become President. Thus, our legislators in the house and senate would have to consider the ramifications if the other party is suddenly in the oval office. Another advantage, if the President and Vice-President, as opposing Parties, can agree on a proposed bill, it might make it easier to get a bill through Congress.

For most of the history of our country, these two top offices have been held by persons of the same party. However, when John Kennedy and Lyndon Johnson, two men from the same Party, were elected, they disliked each other so strongly, they would not even speak to one another. This lack of communication in part led to the escalation of the Viet Nam conflict as well as theories and rumors about Johnson's possible involvement in the Kennedy assassination.

In 1796, John Adams, a Federalist, was elected President and Thomas Jefferson, a Democratic-Republican was elected Vice-President. These two men respected each other, however, they were so opposed to the other's political views they wouldn't support each other.

Another instance was the election of 1800 in which Thomas Jefferson and Aaron Burr, both candidates from the same Party, were tied in the election and it required thirty-six separate votes by Congress to break the deadlock in Jefferson's favor. After Congress decided the election, Jefferson never trusted Burr because of the deceit and dishonesty shown during the campaigning.

People are people and politicians are politicians and it doesn't matter whether they are of the same or opposing party, there will still be issues between them.

Since I'm on the subject of President and Vice-President there are a few issues that need to be addressed as a guidepost to changing how our Government functions

The first is Presidential Security. We all know the Secret Service provides for the personal security of the President. There is also a four-man U.S. Marine detachment assigned to the White House to provide security for the West Wing and to escort the President to and from Marine One and 1300 or more members of the Secret Service "Uniformed Division" (UD) that provide security on the gates and grounds around the White House. One of the largest wastes of tax payer money is the security for the President. I agree that the President needs to be protected wherever he may be, but here's where the waste comes about.

The Marines have been protecting the President and this nation for 227 years. Why is there a need to pay the Secret Service to maintain a special unit to secure the grounds and gates of the White House? The Marines can be taught to do everything the UD does and for a lot less money. The UD falls into the upper level General Schedule. If the Secret Service, Congress or whoever thought up the UD doesn't think the Marines can do the job, then maybe they should go and fight the next war. Please don't misunderstand me, I'm not saying that the UD doesn't do a good job or that the Marines could do a better job. The question is just this, do we need basically three separate entities doing the same job? How many people does it take to change a light bulb? The first waste in Presidential Security is the UD.

The second waste in Presidential Security is the Secret Service personnel that are assigned to protect the vacant homes of the president 24 hours per day/7 days per week/365 days per year. If the President is not in the residence and won't be for months at a time, why keep a security unit there? Send in a clearing unit one or two weeks in advance of the President to make sure that things are in order and safe. There is no need other than Government waste to have a unit securing the house all the time it's vacant. It's no different than the advance unit that clears a hotel the President will stay in while performing a visit away from the White House. If security is so necessary at a President's vacant property, with today's technology it can be monitored by the White House Security Unit. We don't have to have guards on the grounds 24/7/365.

The third waste in Presidential Security is the Secret Service protective unit for former Presidents. When Truman left office, he drove his own car to his home in Missouri. He didn't have a Security detail at his house nor did he have a security detail escorting him home. Once the President leaves office security codes are changed so they can't be compromised and the Former President has no further access to matters of National Security. There is no longer a need for anyone to assassinate them for they no longer have power over the Nation. Why do we spend tax payer money to protect them and all their property for the next ten years or in some cases like Presidents Clinton or Bush, for the rest of their lives?

I've mentioned or hinted at the solution to this waste as I wrote this chapter

1. Stop the protective services for Former Presidents and their property.
2. Stop the protective service for the vacant property of the President.
3. Stop Duplicating Presidential Security. Train the Marines to do the UD job and let them do the job they've done for the past 225 years. Quite frankly most of the world reveres the Marine Corps a lot more than a uniformed police officer. Most people in the United States don't know who the UD is and think of them as Rent-a-Cops. Put a Uniformed Marine on the gate with a 9mm pistol or M-16 rifle and see if the shooting at the guards around the White House subsides. Almost everyone knows that Marines shoot back with deadly accuracy.

RESPONSIBILITIES OF THE PRESIDENT

Article I, Section 7 of the Constitution states that every bill passed by both the House of Representatives and the Senate must be presented to the President for approval. If the President approves the bill, he signs it and it becomes law. If he does not approve the bill, he must formally note his objections and return it to the house where it originated. This is the VETO process. Once the Vetoed bill is returned, it must be reconsidered based on the President's objections then again voted on by both houses – this time requiring a three-quarter majority to pass. In the current party-controlled Congress, it is nearly impossible to gain a three-quarter majority on anything. The big issue of 2014 was whether to allow the construction of the "Keystone" pipeline. Both Houses of Congress passed the bill. President Obama Vetoed it. The people were in favor of the pipeline, and let their Congressional Leaders know it. The President Vetoed it and it was returned to Congress knowing full well the partisan Congress couldn't agree on what color the sky is let alone find a three-quarter majority to overturn the veto.

A little-known fact about the veto process is that the President only has ten days, Sundays excluded, to sign or return a bill. After ten days, the bill becomes law regardless of whether the President approved it. The President can leave a bill sit on his desk for ten days, let it become law and when the public complains about it, he can declare that Congress was to blame because he did not sign it

This section of the Constitution doesn't need to be changed because a good President will use his power of Veto to protect the people and the Constitution. Unfortunately, we haven't had many good Presidents in the past 100 plus years. If we had a good President at any time during the past 100 years, he would have seen the problems and corrected them and I would have very little to write about. Some have come close but all have failed to protect us. What this Section of the Constitution needs is a little work. A little refinement, not rewritten. If the President Veto's a bill, then it should be presented to the people in the next general election to allow the people to formally voice their opinion and concerns. Or, as an alternative have it placed on the State ballots in either the general or special elections. Either of these are viable alternatives to giving the document back to the 535 members of Congress that cannot see past the party line and who do not care about the interests of the people. The popular vote, regardless of the percentage of the voting aged public, would overturn the veto.

The President also has a responsibility to review past and current laws, regulations, bills and mandates for correctness and constitutionality. If he finds that one of these congressional acts needs correction or clarity, he has been granted power by the constitution to enact change. The power of Executive Orders to make the needed correction or give clarity to the document. Executive Orders carry the same weight as Federal law without the vote of Congress or the Senate. Congress and the Senate can overrule and executive order with a two-thirds vote of both houses. An executive order can also be ruled unconstitutional by the Supreme Court.

The Executive Order power was never meant to be Carte Blanche for the President to impose his will on the people or the Government, however, it has been used by several Presidents over our history for just that purpose. Over the last fifty years the excessive use of Executive Orders has created a vast number of problems for both our congressional leaders, the Presidents and the people.

The problem here is that the wording of the Executive Powers doctrine is so vague that like many such documents it is subject to the interpretation of the person reading them. Executive powers have been used by our Presidents to both introduce changes to laws and force their desires upon the nation. The Executive Powers articles need to be refreshed and rewritten in clear enough language to ensure a President cannot abuse this power.

THE SENATE AND HOUSE OF REPRESENTATIVES

Article I of the Constitution defines the three branches of Government. This article originally set forth that the House of Representatives would be elected and that Senators would be appointed. The 17th Amendment changed the rules for Senators, changing them from a gubernatorial appointee to an elected official of the people.

There is a small hiccup in the wording of the Constitution that has been overlooked probably since it was written.

Article I, Section 2 addresses the House and states:

" No Person shall be a Representative who shall not have attained to the Age of twenty-five Years, and been seven years a Citizen of the United States, ***and who shall not, when elected, be an Inhabitant of that State in which he shall be chosen.****"*

And Article I, Section 3 which addresses the Senate also states:

"No Person shall be a Senator who shall not have attained to the Age of thirty Years, and been nine years a Citizen of the United States, ***and who shall not, when elected, be an Inhabitant of that State for which he shall be chosen.****"*

I've highlighted the last part of each sentence because it appears that the men who drafted the Constitution intended that our Senators and Representatives would not be from the State they represent. The word inhabitant is a bit ambiguous. Does it mean that all our elected leaders represent everyone but the State that elects them? Does it mean that the leaders we elect should be from another State? Or, this could be a double negative, in which the meaning would be the opposite of the wording and our leaders will be from the State from which elected.

I only mention this because while our Representatives and Senators are busy trying to change the parts of the Constitution that protect our rights, maybe they should be concentrating on correcting the wording that protects their jobs in sections like this.

The complete Constitution with Amendments is at the end of this book. However, if you want to look it up yourself, just go to the National Archives Website.

Likewise, there should be specific guidelines established for the replacement of representatives who die or resign before the expiration of their elected term.

The reason I bring this up is, in 1960, Keith Thomson, a Republican from Wyoming was elected to the Senate. He died before being sworn in. John Hickey, a Democrat and Governor of Wyoming, appointed himself to fill the vacant Senate Seat until the next general election. It isn't uncommon for this to happen except when the party lines are crossed. Democrat for Republican or vice versa. The People of Wyoming were outraged because Governor Hickey appointed himself. He simply appointed himself and resigned his office.

LOBBY OR BRIBERY?

I originally intended to begin this book with this subject, because this is the key to most activity in Washington, D.C. as well as most lower level governments. However, the preceding chapters won out as the opening chapters and this subject took its more appropriate place.

I will start with a couple of definitions:

Lobby: Per Webster's Dictionary "lobby" is defined as an <u>*attempt*</u> *to influence public officials and legislators.*

Bribery: Webster's Dictionary defines "bribe" as an attempt to corrupt or influence (one in a position of trust) by favors or gifts. Bribery is the act of bribing.

In virtually every country in the world if Favors and Gifts, monetary or otherwise regardless of size or value, are given to a person in Government, it is considered a BRIBE and both the person giving the bribe, and the person receiving the bribe, are sentenced to extended jail time. In some countries, the sentence for bribery is death, since bribery is considered equally heinous to murder, and is a crime against all people. In the United States these favors and gifts or political contributions are considered part of a lobby.

***

There are many ways a member of the legislature can be influenced to vote for or against an issue without the use of bribery. Lobbyists can present signed petitions from the groups they represent identifying public opinion on the issue. They can also present the issue to a congressional board or hearing, showing the relevance of their issue to the public. Neither of these methods incur the use of bribery and these are the methods set forth in our constitution.

***

As I was reading a book titled "Wall Street and The Rise of Hitler" by Antony C. Sutton a very relevant comment in the forward stood out. It basically states that businesses which believe in America don't send lobbyists and administrators to Washington D. C. Those that do send lobbyists are there to manipulate our politicians to their own advantage.

Bribery is illegal even by our laws and should be enforced just as we enforce all other laws. Our elected officials should not be above the law, but should be held accountable for their actions just as We, The People are held accountable for ours. In fact, in 1853 Congress passed laws making bribery of Federal Officers illegal. Yet, throughout the 1900s there were several Congressmen and Senators convicted of bribery, conspiracy to commit bribery or receiving bribes. Some cases being as recent as 1991. What happened to these charges and convictions? Was there any form of punishment? NO! These representatives should have been expelled from Congress and given sentences in jail for no less than one year to be served consecutively for every person in the State, District or region they represented. Many of our elected leaders are guilty of bribery. They are guilty because they pass mandates and laws, that if not accepted or enforced by the States, funding is withheld for roads and health and education. This is a form of bribery. It is also coercion. **Do as we say or else!** They also make deals with the President to pass laws for the people but exempt themselves.

Bribery starts during a campaign for office before the primaries and elections and continues throughout the term of office. Several movies, news articles and political satirists have commented that you cannot spend Millions of Dollars on a campaign and not owe somebody something when it's over. An example of this was Senator Dole who, during his twenty-seven years in the Senate, had spent all his integrity accepting PAC (Political Action Committee) contributions from special interest groups and voting for supporting legislation that gave these special interest groups tax breaks and subsidies far more than the contributions he received. He received $400.000 in campaign contributions from the tobacco industry for claiming that cigarette smoking was not addictive.

In 1907, Congress banned campaign contributions from

Banks and Corporations and in 1943 banned campaign contributions by Labor Unions. How is it, that Senator Dole among others in Congress can receive large contributions from banks, industry and labor unions? Aren't they supposed to be banned? These Bank, Corporate and Labor Union contributions are hidden in the PAC contributions.

A PAC is an organization that collects and pools campaign contributions and donates those contributions to the candidate, ballot initiative or bill they want passed or defeated. Our Representatives are required by law to report campaign contributions and expenditures. They report that they received "X" amount of money from this or that Political Action Committee, PAC. They identify the PAC and the amount received, but there are no regulations requiring the identities of contributors to the PAC. Any time a contribution exceeds $2600 a PAC is formed. PAC contributions line the pockets of almost every political figure in the country; thus, our politicians could be manipulated to repay those contributors in one way shape or form. It could be something as minor and seemingly insignificant as giving the children or relatives of large contributor's positions as aides, secretaries or clerks even though they don't have the skills, knowledge, experience or expertise for the jobs. "You give me your money and support in my campaign and I will provide employment for your working aged children." This would be bribing a contributor by a candidate. Another view would be "I will support your campaign if you give my son-in-law a job as an aide in your office." Tit for Tat or Quid pro quo doesn't work in government because the public is ultimately responsible for paying for whatever the candidate has promised, like the wages for those children or relatives.

If a Representative is treated to a free trip to the Bahamas to meet with a lobbyist group, it is a bribe. Any gift regardless of size or value given by any group to a Representative of the Government should be considered a bribe. The only exception would be a Christmas or Birthday card if there wasn't any value other than the card itself and the stamp to mail it. Special Interest Groups, Big Bank and Big Industry and Labor Unions are not in the business of investing gifts and favors or campaign contributions without expecting some type of return on that investment.

Any Government official that violates the law should be prosecuted to the fullest extent of the law and be sentenced to the maximum punishment for their crime. They are, after all, representing the entire jurisdiction of their position. Therefore, any crime committed is a crime against all the people of their district or state. Any official suspected of a crime should be immediately suspended from office until an independent investigation can be conducted by some entity who is not a member of Congress. If charged and found guilty of a crime, that representative should be permanently removed and replaced by a representative of the same party affiliation and appointed by the Governor of the State. The Governor should not appoint themselves. This appointee would serve out the remaining term of the guilty elected person. If a member is expelled from Congress, they should not be eligible to run again for any public office.

Here's a bit of trivia and something that needs to be addressed and laws passed to prevent it from happening again. In 1967 Adam Clayton Powell Jr (D) was expelled from Congress following allegations of corruption, but was allowed to run again in the Special election for his replacement. He won and was elected as his own replacement.

We, The People, meaning all the people of the country, must take an active interest in what our government and elected officials are doing and start making our representatives **"toe the line"**.

In 1921, Congress established the Government Accounting Office (GAO) to audit and investigate Government. This Government agency has performed their job well and in past years has saved the taxpayers billions of dollars; however, our elected leaders do not always follow the recommendations of the GAO and continue to waste those same tax dollars.

In 1925, Congress passed the Corrupt Practices Act which limited Campaign expenditures - another Law that needs a tune-up. If we have laws that limit how much a candidate can spend on a campaign – how are our candidates able to continually spend millions of dollars on their campaigns?

One way to ensure that our representatives are working for us would be to pass legislation allowing the people to fire them. The problem with this type of regulation would be to determine what percentage of the population would have to agree and how to get that number accounted for without having annual, quarterly or even monthly election type consensus reviews. Even then, how would we remove them from office? What would be the method for installing a temporary replacement?

I'm sure there are enough under-employed Federal workers and IRS Agents that could be assigned to assist the GAO in investigating and auditing the financial records and accounts of our elected officials annually. The downside of these investigations would be that any monetary bribery would then be redirected to untraceable off-shore accounts in alias names for those officials and contributors who choose to violate the law. If the official will break the law to accept the bribe, they will break the law to hide it.

As it is now, any person holding a political position, regardless of the level of Government, can be the subject of "bribery" and very few of our officials whether elected or appointed leave their positions in the same or worse financial condition than they were when they assumed the position. Maybe they should assume another position, one commanded by law enforcement. The only way a Representative should ever leave office as a millionaire, is if they were millionaires before entering office or have very good investment and or money management programs funded by their own money not the money given them by lobbyists.

If you feel that your representative is guilty of accepting bribes or in any way not representing you, Vote them out of office.

How do we fix the bribery? We have Laws in place to prevent bribery, but we allow the PAC contributions, and lobbyist's gifts, which are plain and simple bribery.

Here's a solution:

1. Enforce the Congressional ban of contributions from Banks, Corporations and unions. Give the GAO teeth and make them responsible for the enforcement and prosecute representatives and industries that violate the law.

2. Ban campaign contributions from Political Action Committees or make them disclose every contributor to ensure that Banks, Corporations and Unions are not using them to hide their contributions and influence our representatives and again make the GAO responsible for enforcement of the ban.

3. Enforce the Corrupt Practices Act and set realistic limits on campaign expenditures. Once again give the GAO enforcement responsibility.

4. Pass a law that all campaign contributions must be submitted to the U.S. Treasury in the name of the candidate being supported. The Treasury will set up a special account for each candidate's contributions and with the assistance of the GAO will ensure that Banks, Corporations and Unions are not contributors. Likewise,

State or Local Candidates, like the Governor or Mayor, would have their political contributions go to the State or Local Treasury in their name. No contribution for any political campaign may be given directly to the candidate.

5. The Treasury issues the candidate a debit card with a limit of the funds available in their contributions account for use during the campaign, not to exceed the limit set by the Corrupt Practices Act.

6. Once the candidate is defeated any residual funds in the account will be transferred to the general fund and used toward paying the National Debt.

7. If a candidate is elected, the funds will remain in their account and be added to any contributions for future reelection campaigns. Any interest gained by these accounts will be channeled to the general fund for payment on the National Debt.

8. If a candidate chooses not to campaign for further office or has reached their maximum term of office, the funds will be transferred to the general fund for payment on the National Debt.

9. Any Politician found accepting personal contributions in a manner other than as described above will be prosecuted for accepting bribes and the contributor will be prosecuted for bribery.

10. Each candidate for political office must file a financial declaration showing all personal and family assets prior to announcing their candidacy. A candidate may use personal and family monetary funds without restriction, but must account for any gains, of any amount, to personal or family wealth.

Since we obviously cannot rely on our representatives not to accept bribes, then we must establish criteria to ensure their contributions are used for pursuing the political office and not for lining their pockets. We can attempt to prevent our representatives from accepting bribes from special interest groups by making it more difficult to do so, but, unfortunately, there will still be those who will try.

"If, to please the people, we offer what we ourselves disapprove, how can we afterwards defend our work? Let us raise a standard to which the wise and the honest can repair. The event is in

the hand of God." – George Washington to the First Continental Congress, May 1787.

President Washington was saying that Congress must be true to themselves. How can they vote the party line for a special interest project or bill which they personally feel isn't in the best interest of the country and still defend that bill to their constituents who believe these leaders will do the correct thing to represent them?

NOT ABOVE THE LAW

Throughout our Nation's history there have been members of Congress who felt they were above the law because they were the ones who wrote the laws. There have been members of both houses of Congress who believed their jobs were Constitutional – they worked for the Constitution not the people. Sorry folks, the document – The Constitution – defines your job just like any other job description. It does not hire you, it does not pay you nor does it exempt you from Law or legal prosecution. If you believe you work for the Constitution, then let that document pay your salary and take that burden off the taxpayer. Please, see how much money comes out of the sealed case which houses the U.S. Constitution.

The Capitol Police Department was established in 1800. Beginning as Security Guards for the Capitol and Congressional Chambers, their Primary function was to protect the Capitol and other buildings occupied by the Federal Government as well as the people who worked within those buildings. Over the past two centuries they have become a legitimate Police Department.

There have been instances where Capitol Police Officers have stopped members of Congress to prevent them from driving while intoxicated only to be reprimanded by their superiors, made to apologize and/or have been fired from their position. They were trying to do their job – protecting the Government property, the representatives and the public. Why were these intoxicated members of Congress on the property? Could it be they were engaged in some business other than representing the people? There are numerous times when Capitol Police have found our representatives having parties and sex with staffers and aides in the representative's office, in conference rooms, hallways, closets, the various passages and even on the steps to the Capitol. Many of these encounters were never reported by the Capitol Police. The Halls of Congress are not our representative's personal playground. They are owned by the taxpaying people who have voted those representatives into office expecting them to uphold a certain amount of professional and moral standards and decorum.

In one case in the early 1980s, a staff secretary entered a House of Representatives building with a loaded weapon. A police officer confiscated the weapon and the woman made such a fuss that the supervisor came out to see what the problem was. The supervisor called the Representative the woman worked for, Congressman Newt Gingrich. Mr. Gingrich came to the police office and demanded the weapon be returned to the woman and that she be allowed to continue to her place of work. Mr. Gingrich later issued a statement that he owned the weapon although the woman had already confessed to owning it to the police. The weapon was returned to the woman. Regardless of who owned the gun, it was concealed in the woman's purse and conveyed into a Government building. Carrying a concealed weapon is a criminal offense in Washington D.C. and Carrying a weapon into a Government building is a Federal offense. Neither the Representative nor the woman were ever charged. The Officer that confiscated the weapon was fired. Many time people were arrested for carrying weapons into the various Capitol buildings, depending on who you were no reports were made or cases prosecuted.

In 1890, Capitol Police were forced to intensify Security procedures to include a "NO Weapons allowed" policy after a Senator was shot by a journalist inside the Capitol. The procedures were changed again after Capitol bombings in 1971 and 1995.

Where do our representatives get the idea that because of who they are they are above the law? The Constitution protects representatives who are on their way to or from Congressional Chambers or present in Chambers during a session. It does not allow them to blatantly disregard the law any time they choose. This is another place where the wording but not the intent of the Constitution needs some refinement.

HOMESTEADING IN GOVERNMENT

"Politicians are like diapers; they need to be changed often and for the same reason." – Mark Twain.

I think Mark Twain has put the homesteading subject in the best possible perspective.

One of the largest problems with our current government is the fact that once a person is elected to office, unless they are voted out, they can, if reelected, stay in that office until they chose to retire or die. A prime example of this is Tipp O'Neal (D) who served in the House of Representatives for thirty-four years and was the Speaker of the House for ten of those years. His dedication to the Party line and being in office for that long gave him power over the junior representatives from both parties. Very few would oppose him on any issue. He could easily influence Congress to vote with him on any number of issues even if those issues weren't in the best interest of the people.

After World War II, Congress saw that there could be a problem with the President serving multiple terms of office. Franklin D. Roosevelt had served as President from 1933 until his death in April of 1945, twelve years in Office and the longest tenure of any President before or after him. Adolf Hitler was Chancellor of Germany from 1933 until his death in April of 1945. Although, these two men had similar political careers, both were dedicated to their countries and both died in office, they were very different in personalities. Both Roosevelt and Hitler had definite plans for bringing their countries out of the Great Depression. It was Hitler's early economic policies that made Germany the forerunner of economic recovery and gained him support from Wall Street. President Roosevelt was not far behind, but had a much larger country and more diverse demographics to consider.

Congress recognized that if the persona had been reversed, the country could have been under a dictator for many years. In 1947, Congress proposed an amendment to limit the President to two terms of office totaling eight years, thus protecting us from being ruled by a dictator. The proposal was ratified in 1951 and became the 22nd Amendment, but the constitutional amendment placed no restrictions on the terms of Congress. In other words, the 22nd Amendment may have protected us from one tyrant, but gave away that protection to 535 tyrants (members of Congress), by allowing them to serve many terms of office and it is Congress that writes and passes the laws of the country, not the President.

Longevity in office, is a curse to the public. If we don't change our representatives frequently, then we don't have change in the way government thinks. No new blood, means no new incentive or new thought of how we can do better. Government becomes status quo. Even though we may elect a few new members periodically, the larger group has been and remains in office for decades. While experience may be beneficial in most businesses, in Government, it tends to lend itself more to stagnation. The "Good Ole Boy" system takes over and those that have been tenured in office tend to seek out their like-minded senior representatives to vote for or against proposed bills regardless of costs to the people. By not seeking out the newer representatives they fail to get the additional insight the newly elected representative may have to offer. This "Good Ole Boy" network also gives way to vote trading. One representative will agree to vote for another's bill if that representative agrees to vote for theirs. Again quid pro quo does not work in government. This not only applies to our elected representatives in both the federal and state governments, but also to our city and county elected officials and our Federal Judges who are currently appointed for life. After hearing the same variety of cases year in and year out, Judges tend to stagnate in their decisions on the cases they hear, adjudicating them with basically the same judgment each time. In Federal Court because of the long-term Brotherhood of Judges and the "Good Ole Boy" network, vote trading is rampant. Replacing them frequently helps to prevent the trading of rulings and the "television Judge" mentality.

Our elected officials were never supposed to be career positions. The men that drafted the Constitution and Bill of Rights for this country intended that our representatives would serve the country for their terms, possibly thinking of one or two terms and then go home to attend to their businesses or farms. Our elected officials weren't supposed to make more than the median income of those they represent, but today they make tenfold the median income of their represented areas.

Thomas Jefferson said *"The tree of liberty must be refreshed from time to time with the blood of patriots and tyrants."* This colloquialism didn't mean that we should have revolution, but we need to refresh our leaders often to prevent the need for revolution.

Many people believe that no representative should serve more that the term that has been established for the President. The men who drafted the Constitution believed there had to be a stability in Government – a House, in this case the Senate, which could continue to govern even in election years when it was anticipated there would be a major turnover in the House of Representatives

Here's a solution:

1. No Elected Official should serve longer than TEN (10) years total in any office or combination of offices.
2. A Congressman is elected for two years. We need to change this to four years with one-half of the House being elected every two years. If the current system terms of office are used, they can be re-elected five times or may run for Senate or President, but they cannot run for election or reelection to any office that would allow them to serve more than the ten-year maximum.
3. A Senator, on the other hand, is elected for six years. They cannot be reelected to the Senate; however, they can run for the House or President but they cannot run for election or reelection to any office that would allow them to serve more than the ten-year maximum.
4. City and County officials and Judges should be held to the same ten-year restriction. Stagnation is the same regardless of the level of government.
5. Federal Judges should be elected by the people just as our State, County and City Judges are. The President may select the candidates for Federal Judge and the Senate approves the candidate selected, but the people decide whether they should serve in Federal Court.

"The power under the constitution will always be in the people. It is entrusted for certain defined purposes, and for a certain limited period, to representatives of their own choosing; and, whenever it is executed contrary to their interest, or not agreeable to

their wishes, their servants can and undoubtedly will be recalled." –
George Washington

"However, [political parties] may now and then answer popular ends, they are likely in the course of time and things, to become potent engines, by which cunning, ambitious, and unprincipled men will be enabled to subvert the power of the people and to usurp for themselves the reins of government, destroying afterwards the very engines which have lifted them to unjust dominion." – George Washington Farewell Address 1796

KEEPING THE PUBLIC INFORMED
RESPONSIBILITY AND ACCOUNTABILITY

"Knowledge is in every country the surest basis of public happiness."
– George Washington Speech to Congress, Jan 1790

It is imperative that our representatives keep us informed of what they are doing in our Government. If we are not kept informed by our representatives, then our only source of knowledge comes from a tainted press. I say tainted press because the news agencies seem to swing either liberal or conservative like the flag in the wind, blowing whichever way gives the least resistance and makes the bigger news story.

Many, but not all, representatives publish news letters to their districts explaining what is happening in Government and asking for feedback on what the district feels is the popular way to vote. Unfortunately, many of those representatives only send newsletters to the registered voters of their party. They should be sending those newsletters to every person in the district. A great number of the requests for input or feedback go unanswered until after the vote when the people are angered by the law or bill that was just passed. Even with Email, the voice of the people isn't measured accurately because of the vast number of people that either don't have computers, can't afford an internet source, don't want the technology or simply don't want to get involved.

Our representatives must keep us informed. They must use every medium available, News, Email, newsletters and public assemblies in their districts. Each member of Congress has an office that is staffed and maintained somewhere in their district. These offices and staff people should be out talking to the people on the issues being addressed in Congress. We pay these people to support our representatives, they should be working for their pay by doing more than fielding phone calls and opening mail to shield the representative from the public they serve. The telephone has been so over-used and abused in past elections that most people just hang up as soon as the recorded message starts and identifies the call as anything political, they are a complete waste of time and money. Another waste of time and money are political flyers. These flyers are also overused and abused during elections and most end up in the trash before being read. Flyers, phone calls, even newsletters and email need to express their purpose as wanting the public's opinion on legislation that is before Congress and this expression must be fore-front on the document. How many blocks per day could be canvased door to door?

Two former longtime Republican leaders, Senator Everett Dirksen and Representative Charlie Halleck would go on television and tell the people what was happening in Washington D.C. Often seen together and with such frequency that the press jokingly dubbed their appearances "The Ev and Charlie Show". They not only kept their districts and states informed, but the rest of the country as well.

There are a vast number of people in the United States who are fed up with the "Status Quo" of government. Thus, they have just tune out anything about the Government. Others feel so meaningless and helpless, they have also tuned Government out. Approximately thirty-six percent of the population are elderly and have given up on ever being able to do anything to change Government.

Ladies and Gentlemen: It's time to tune Government back in and take an active stand to make it work for us. **You Can Make a Difference!** You can group together with your neighbors, and friends to make your local community representatives **"Toe the Line."** By increasing the size of your group with the aid of those community leaders, you can force change in your City Government representatives -- then County, State and Federal representatives, at each level building a stronger and more vocal group until all our representatives "Toe the Line" since they are, in effect, our employees.

If you don't feel like your representative is keeping you up to date on the issues, confront them and let them know that you are to be informed. Don't be a mushroom, kept in the dark and fed manure!

Our elected representatives have a single responsibility. To represent the people! They must be held accountable for that responsibility. If they fail in their responsibility to the people, they should be removed from office, either by voting them out or by calling for a congressional hearing to dismiss them.

"The best way to preserve the confidence of the people durably is to promote their true interests." – George Washington 1780

ATTENDANCE AND VOTING RECORDS

Attendance has always been a big issue with our Representatives and, to some degree, attendance falls back to the chapter on pay. We pay our representatives to do a job for us, but if they do not attend the congressional meetings and do not vote, what are we paying them for. We often see pictures of the Senate and or House of Representatives on CNN, CSPAN or whatever Congressional Channel you get in your area, and the seats are virtually empty. You see more people in Colorado ski resorts during the summer months.

It is not important for our Representatives to be in their respective chambers every day, because they have other business researching bills, drafting 200 Amendments to the Constitution, reinventing the wheel, mandating the menu of the cafeteria and finding better ways to avoid serving the people they represent. As I said in the Forward of this book, the House and Senate propose about 200 Amendments to the Constitution during each 2-year term of Congress. Boys and Girls, with very few exceptions, the Constitution is just fine. **Leave it alone.**

It is important, however, that our Senators and Congressmen and Women be in attendance during those times when Congress is convened for the purpose of passing legislation. The absence of a single vote can change the passage of a bill from opposed, to approved or to opening a filibuster. For those of you who may not be familiar with a filibuster, it is a deadlock, an action that delays or obstructs progress in a legislative assembly. Filibusters were originally introduced to Congress in 1880 and are usually started when a party or group of representatives is so opposed to a certain bill they give exceedingly long speeches thus delaying or obstructing the Congress from voting or proceeding to other business. At times, these speeches prevent others from taking the floor and often do not even touch the bill being presented.

Voting records which show how all the representatives voted in both the House and Senate are part of the public record. Their attendance record is also available in the public record. If you don't want to spend hours searching the public records, there are Watch Dog groups in just about every state that constantly monitor your representatives voting record. We have all had our fill of political campaign junk mail providing information about a candidate's voting record on controversial subjects and their absence during sessions of Congress. The bulk of that information is collected by watch dog organizations. There are Republican, Democrat and independent groups all watching our representatives and collecting as much information as they can for their party so they have plenty of information for the next election campaign. The problem with a party-affiliated watch dog organization is that they are generally swayed toward their party. If someone of their party is absent from a meeting, they will say that representative was engaged in State business. But if the representative is from the opposing party they will count them as absent even if the representative only missed the roll call. The public record shows if the person came in late after the roll call was taken. A few States have watch dog groups which aren't related to party affiliations but just collect the information for public awareness. They aren't listed in the phone book as "political watch dog". They will be listed as such and such for awareness, or something about need to know. There are as many different names as there are organizations.

This Chapter is for information more than presenting solutions. Our Representatives are constantly under the microscope by some Watch Dog organization or another through the public record. We need to be aware of what our representatives are doing. Why were they absent from a legislative meeting? Were they back in the state campaigning? Were they on a lobbyist junket? Were they shaking hands with people from the State getting input and feedback? Were they drafting an Amendment to the Constitution? What were they doing?

If they are not doing the job they were hired to do, then why are we paying them. Their pay should be docked for the hours missed during the session. A missed session would mean that the representative not only missed roll call but was absent for the entire proceeding.

If they were not in their chair during the legislative session, then they were not performing the job they were hired to do.

If you are concerned about the attendance and voting record of your representative, check them out.

If you feel they are not doing what you hired them to do, Vote them out.

Solutions:

1. Remove Filibustering from Congress and establish a severe fine for those who attempt it.
2. Require that all Representatives be in attendance when there is a bill on the agenda, including the Omnibus appropriations bill. It is important that every member of Congress and the Senate be present to vote.
3. Make every Congressperson responsible and accountable to the people they represent. If they are absent from a vote, they must be required to formally explain why and where they were.

GOVERNMENT PROPERTY

With each new change of Congressional leader, change of Command in the Military, and Presidential turn over, the new person wants to remodel to brighten up, freshen up or refurnish their office or offices.

This must stop! These offices are not theirs, **they are ours.** The Offices, the furnishings, the Government Services Agency (GSA) vehicles and all other Government property belongs to us, the people of the United States. We paid for it. Millions of dollars are spent each year on furnishings and adornments for which taxpayers pay.

An example of this waste is the recent remodeling of the foyer outside of the office of a General at the Air Force Academy in Colorado Springs. The cost of the remodel was $387,000.00 about $130,000.00 more than the average cost of a home in the community. This was just the foyer to the offices, not the entire office building. Remember, Government contracts are supposed to be awarded to the lowest bidder, but who is watching to see that these bids on contracts are not inflated above the community average for the type of work. The cost of this foyer remodel was approved by a committee and the pentagon, but who's money was used for this extremely expensive remodel? **The taxpayers.**

Here's a simple solution for this problem:

1.   An inventory of furnishings should be made of each room or office where a person may be assigned.
2.   Each person assigned a room or office must carefully inventory the overall condition of the room or office and the furnishings within it before occupying the space.
3.   No furniture can be purchased or remodeling by the Government within ten years of the last purchase or remodel for that space. The exception would be to replace

broken or damaged items.

4. An exit inventory, including overall condition of the space and furnishings will be conducted prior to evacuating the space.

5. Any damage other than normal wear and tear will be the responsibility of the person who has occupied that space.

6. If a person has furniture from their previous office, they may bring that furniture to the Government office space and it will be noted on the inventory as personally owned property. If the person wants to refurnish the office at their expense, all Government property will be placed in suitable storage for the next tenant. The Building Manager must ensure that these stored furnishings are returned to the office space from which they originated upon receipt of an exit inventory from the tenant that had them removed.

This is our property, the President, Congress, Generals or any other Civil or Military Person is basically renting that space from us. They are responsible for taking care of the space as well as the contents within it.

As for GSA vehicles, I have driven my own car to and from work, on trips and all over town since I've could drive. Why do we have to maintain a fleet of GSA vehicles for our Government? They are perfectly able to drive themselves and their own vehicles anywhere they want to go. Senator O'Mahoney drove himself in his own car to work every day he was in office. When he traveled, he paid for his own rental vehicles. When his wife had a stroke requiring nursing care around the clock, the Senator paid for the nurse out of his own pocket and bought a second car and hired a driver to be available to transport his wife to the store and doctor's appointments, again out of his own pocket. The only vehicles that should be maintained by the Government at any level are Military, Law Enforcement which includes Border Patrol, Forest and National Park Services and the Presidential Limo and Security escort vehicles. It is a whole lot cheaper for the tax payer to reimburse the thirty-five cents a mile for travel than to purchase and maintain a fleet of vehicles. This goes for State, County, City and other local Governments as well. Why does an urban police force need to have big gas sucking SUVs as patrol units? It's not like they need to go four wheeling anywhere. For supervisors and investigators there may be a need for a larger vehicle because of the extra equipment they need to perform their job, but not for urban patrol units.

If we do not question our Government officials, they will continue to think they are in control of us, not that they work for us.

THE ARMED FORCES, VETERANS AND THEIR BENEFITS

"There is nothing so likely to produce peace as to be well prepared to meet an enemy." –George Washington Jan 1780.

President Washington's statement has been proven time and time again as the United States Military has answered the call to arms.

The United States Military is constantly training for and being deployed to conflicts around the world. Our Soldiers, Sailors, Airmen and Marines took an oath to **Support and Defend** our Country and the Constitution against all Enemies Foreign and Domestic. We have been deployed into conflicts around the world as the world's peace keepers. We have taken up arms against our own citizens during riots. Yet members of our Government are continually trying to reduce the size of the Military as well as Pay, Veteran's Benefits and Retirement.

The young men and women in the military are Patriots. Yes, many have joined for the educational benefits of the GI Bill or technical skills training they could not otherwise afford in a civilian school; but they serve and go where they are told to go by the same Government that wants to reduce their funding. Many of those young Soldiers, Sailors, Marines and Airmen who follow the decrees of our Government never return home, and many more that do return have permanent mental and physical scars that haunt their very existence and cut deep into their souls for the rest of their lives and yet there are still members of Government that want to reduce benefits to these noble Warriors and Patriots.

The Constitution of 1789 gives Congress the authority to maintain a strong military for the National Defense. Today, Congress will bypass and usurp the Constitution for their own greed and gain and want to weaken the Military by reducing pay and benefits and funding needed to provide for a strong National Defense. Our Congress says they need to reduce military pay and benefits to be able to research and build items that will reduce casualties on the battle field. Then they will vote against funding for those very items they cut the pay and benefits for.

Let's take a little Quiz:
Can you name this Country?
It has the following:
709,000 Regular (Active Duty) Troops
293,000 Reserve Troops
8 Army Divisions
20 Air Force and Navy Air Wings with 2000 Combat Aircraft
232 Strategic Bombers
19 Strategic Missile Submarines
4 Aircraft Carriers
121 Surface Warships with support bases, shipyards and logistical assets to support this sized naval force.

If you are having trouble naming the country that would have all of this, you are not alone. You see these aren't the Military Assets of a foreign country. These are United States Military forces and assets that were eliminated during the Clinton Administration and each year our Government wants to reduce them further and cut more benefits.

The Continental Congress of 1776 established the first benefits for Veterans providing benefits for Disabled Veterans and Direct Medical and Hospital Care. In 1834 the benefit was expanded to include widows and dependents of Veterans. In 1917 Congress established a new program for Veterans, but it was administered by three different branches of Government. These administrative duties were consolidated into the Veteran's Administration (VA) in 1930. Each year Congress votes to change how Veterans are viewed by the VA. In the beginning, the VA provided benefits to only active duty Veterans or those with 181 consecutive days of active duty with a Service Related injury or disability. If a Veteran had a Service Related injury or disability all treatment at a VA facility was at no cost to the Veteran. However, not all Veterans were eligible. You had to be able to prove your service and prove that any ailment or injury was "Service Related." A Friend of mine served in the Army from 1944, the last year of WWII, until his enlistment was up in 1948. He stayed in the Army Reserve and was recalled to active duty in 1951 for service in the Korean War and served until 1958. During his service in WWII he was wounded and has an inoperable piece of shrapnel in his back next to his spinal cord. Although he has awards and medals including a Purple Heart, he cannot prove that he served in the military or that his injury was Service Related. The Army Records Center had a major fire and burned down in 1973 and his records were lost. To date, at 90 years old, he has not been afforded the Veteran's benefits he has earned and still carries the shrapnel in his back with no compensation from the Government. This is one example among approximately 18 million Veterans whose records were lost in the fire. The fire in 1973, occurring at the end of the Vietnam Conflict when many Veterans were experiencing problems that are related to Agent Orange, has brought up many good questions. Were the records intentionally burned to allow Government to avoid paying benefits to the veterans of the previous four wars? Some of these Veterans were admitted into the VA system before the fire, however, because their records were destroyed, it is difficult to prove the Service relationship of their injuries and cannot receive any increase to the treatment or disability pension they were originally placed on. A good many more records were lost in the several floods and natural disasters that have inundated the St Louis, Mo area, but many of these records were on microfilm, so they could be recovered. We cannot blame Acts of God like fire and flood on Congress, but taking care of our Veterans is another thing entirely. What are we doing for the 18 million Veterans who lost records in the fire? **Nothing!** What are we doing for Veterans as a whole? **Very Little!**

The Serviceman's Readjustment Act of 1944, created the GI Bill, provided money for Veterans to go to school and obtain an education that would help them compete in the civilian work force. These Veterans also received unemployment benefits, full tuition including books and fees, as well as money for living expenses. They were given access to home and small business loans to help them become recognized members of their communities. Veterans didn't have to contribute to this plan because they have already contributed their lives to this country's defense instead of going to college right out of High School. Many of this Veterans didn't voluntarily enlist in the Military. From the end of World War II in 1945 through the end of the Viet Nam Conflict in 1975 there were hundreds of thousands of young men who were drafted. Conscripted into Military Service by our Government and a forgotten when they return home. Many historians and economists attribute the GI Bill with being a key factor in America's post WW II economic growth.

In 1952, the Veterans Readjustment Act replaced the earlier Serviceman's Act and reduced the benefits which had been received by the WWII Vets. The new bill no longer paid unemployment benefits or significantly reduced unemployment benefits after a waiting period. Veterans no longer received living expenses or full tuition with books and fees. Instead, they received $110.00 per month with which they paid for their tuition, books, fees and living expenses.

These two versions of the GI Bill provided benefits for only those Veterans who served during time of war (WWII and Korea) and did not provide any type of benefit for those who served in non-combative roles or during the peacetime years.

Between 1956 and 1966, there were many bills and debates in Congress to change the GI Bill to include benefits for all Veterans whether the conditions were war or peacetime; finally gaining full support of Congress in 1966 and being signed into law as the Veterans Readjustment Act of 1966 by President Lyndon Johnson. The initial bill reduced the benefit to $100.00 for living expenses, tuition, books and fees which many Veteran's Groups protested as being too low. The $100 would barely cover the cost of books. The amount was increased several times until the Readjustment Assistance Act of 1972 was passed which maintained a cost of living increase each year.

In 1976 Congress passed the Veterans Education Assistance Program (VEAP) and Montgomery GI Bill. VEAP required Military to contribute to their education and the program would match those funds two to one meaning the GI Bill would pay $2.00 for every $1.00 contributed by the Serviceman. If the Veteran had not contributed they would have no benefit which was bad for both the Veteran and the economy of the nation. During the years of VEAP military pay was so low that many couldn't afford to contribute very much to the program. Veterans that had been grandfathered into the 1966 and 1972 acts were still able to maintain their benefits under those acts but had to use them by 1986 or lose them. Many Senior Non-Commissioned Officers (NCOs) and Officers left the service to use their benefits which left a rift in the experience level of the military. Those that remained lost their 1972 benefits and became eligible for the Montgomery GI Bill (MGIB). The MGIB requires that a Service Member forfeit $100 of their pay per month during their first twelve months of Service. They must use the Educational benefits within 10 years of their enlistment date or loose the benefit including the $1200 forfeited to have the benefit. Basically, our Military members are being taxed $1200 for their GI Bill Educational benefits, and if they decide to make a career of the military or otherwise don't use the benefit, they have lost that contribution. If they use the benefit they receive approximately $1600 per month for 36 months, a total of $57,600, while attending school full time. There is a Buy-up option where a Service member can forfeit up to $600 per month for the first twelve months of enlistment and will receive $150 for thirty-six months for an additional total of $5400. Let's see how the buy-up works out; the soldier contributes $600 per month for twelve months a total of $7200 and receives $5400 in benefits in return. If we take the total benefit the government pays approximately $63,000 over thirty-six months. With surmounting educational costs this figure if paid directly to the school would cover about four semesters or two years of College without the summer session. If the Soldier chooses not to attend the summer session, he will not receive benefits and must reapply for benefits when he returns in the fall. At any rate the Soldier is still two years from being able to complete his bachelor's education on the GI Bill. Consider this, the service person must contribute $600 for the first 12 months of their enlistment. An E-1, basic entry rate for all Military, receives only $1599 per month. Granted that these servicemen and women have basically no expenses, but asking them to give up a third of their pay for the little benefit is ludicrous at best.

I've shown where Congress has steadily decreased the value of the GI Bill but they haven't stopped there. They have reduced the amount of Healthcare coverage provided to Veteran Retirees and raised their premiums, while creating a Veterans Administration that routinely disapproves applications of Veterans with "Service Connected" disabilities, that charges co-pays for treatment at VA facilities and ignores or postpones treatment for Veterans who need the help. Twenty-Two Veterans commit suicide every day, yet the VA has not created a positive support unit for these troubled Vets. What is our Government doing about this? **Nothing!** They are too busy trifling and bickering over Gun Control, same sex marriage, and abortion legislation. Why haven't they dedicated any money toward the problem of Veteran Benefits? Because Our Elected Leaders are too busy kissing ass to party lines to consider what's good for the

Country, their Constituents or the Veterans who have kept us safe and free and those elected leaders in office.

In 2012, I wrote an email to the Senator from New Mexico regarding the changes to reduce retiree health insurance benefits and the rise in the cost of premiums to which this Senator responded that the reason for the changes was so the Government could spend more money researching and developing drone technology to save lives on the battle fields of the future. He said basically that the changes to Tricare were necessary to save the defense budget 17.6 billion dollars over the next five years to offset the 486.8 billion the Government was spending in 2012 on modernization of the Military. Somehow the math just doesn't add up, much like the rest of Government's math. Seventeen billion dollars over 5 year to offset a $486 billion-dollar spending deficit in 2012. I reminded the Senator that this country has been blessed by the men and women who have stood the ground and that, in battle, you can have all the smart technology in the world but until you have boots on the ground you don't hold the property. It's like flying over New Mexico, you may find a nice-looking piece of property but until you stand on it, it's not yours. I also let him know that I was sending the entire email conversation to everyone I knew. He never responded again.

Bottom line, we must provide for a strong National Defense and we need to take care of our Veterans who provide that defense. It is their courage and commitment to this country that has kept us free. Our Military Men and Women take an Oath to Support and Defend the United States and the Constitution against ALL Enemies, Foreign and Domestic. We may have threats from foreign powers but the biggest threat to America's Freedom and our way of life is the domestic threat of our own Government.

WORLD HERITAGE SITES AND BIOSPHERE RESERVES

Many people are completely unaware that our National Parks have been turned over to the United Nations to control. Our Founding Fathers would be rolling in their graves to learn their successors have turned over large pieces of American Sovereign Soil to other nations.

In 1972, Our Government and President Nixon signed the World Heritage Treaty, a Treaty which creates World Heritage Sites and Biosphere Reserves. These World Heritage Sites are monitored and governed by the United Nations Educational, Scientific and Cultural Organization (UNESCO). The sites were selected for their cultural, historical or natural significance.

National Governments are mandated by UNESCO to protect these sites. Through this international treaty, the United States Government is allowing the United Nations and its member Countries access and control of American Territory.

U. S. Sites currently monitored by UNESCO include but are not limited to:

Cultural Sites
Cahokia Mounds State Historical Site,
        Missouri (1982)
Chaco Cultural, Arizona, New Mexico,
        Colorado, Utah (1987)
Independence Hall, Pennsylvania (1979)
La Fortaleza and San Juan M=National
        Historic Site, Puerto Rico (1983)
Mesa Verde National Park, Colorado (1978)
Monticello and University of Virginia,
        Charlottesville, Virginia (1987)

Monumental Earthworks of Poverty Point,
    Louisiana
San Antonio Missions, Texas (2015)
Statue of Liberty, New York, New Jersey
    (1984)
Taos Pueblo, Arizona, New Mexico (1992)

Natural Sites
Carlsbad Caverns, New Mexico (1995)
Everglades National Park (1979)
Grand Canyon National park, Arizona (1979)
Great Smokey Mountains National Park,
    Tennessee, N. Carolina (1983)
Hawaii Volcanoes National Park, Hawaii
    (1987)
Glacier Bay, Alaska (1995)
Mammoth Cave National Park, Kentucky
    (1981)
Olympic National Park, Washington State
    (1981)
Redwood National and State Parks, California
    (1980)
Watertown Glacier International Peace Park,
    Montana, Canada (1995)
Yellowstone National Park, Wyoming,
    Montana (1978)
Yosemite National Park, California (1984)

Properties on the Tentative list.
Civil Rights Movement sites, Alabama (2008)
Dayton Aviation sites, Ohio (2008)
Hopewell Ceremonial Earthworks, Ohio
    (2008)
Thomas Jefferson Buildings, Virginia (2008)
Mount Vernon, Virginia (2008)
Serpent Mound, Ohio (2008)
Frank Lloyd Wright Buildings, Arizona,
    California, Illinois, New York,
    Oklahoma, Pennsylvania, Wisconsin (2008)
Fagatele Bay National Marine Sanctuary,
    American Samoa (2008)

Okefenoke National Wildlife Refuge, Georgia
(2008)
Petrified Forest National Park, Arizona, (2008)
White Sands National Monument, New
Mexico (2008)

On Tentative List without dates of submission
The Washington Monument
The Brooklyn Bridge

The dates behind the names on this list are the dates these sites were added to the UNESCO World Heritage Site list.

All together 68 percent of all American National Parks and Monuments are controlled by the United Nations. This number is correct as of 2015 when I first published this book. President Obama submitted many more of our parks and landmarks for tentative inclusion on the World Heritage List during his administration.

We are required to maintain these UNESCO controlled parks and spaces yet, we receive no aid for the upkeep from them to do so. However, through various UNESCO mandates, many are being closed to the public or have very restricted public access. What were open public lands, are no longer public but have exorbitant fees which continually rise. Hiking trails and campgrounds have been closed. Public Access has been made illegal with threats of being prosecuted for trespassing.

Wait a minute, isn't this our country? Aren't we, the tax payers, still paying for the upkeep and maintenance? Yet we cannot have access to these National Landmarks. It goes much further than that.

In 1995, UNESCO had listed Yellowstone National Park as a World Heritage Site in Danger. Meaning that the site must be closely monitored to insure there is no further damage or erosion of the site.

A small mining company in Montana was forced to abandon a mine development project because of its proximity to Yellowstone National Park. Mining isn't unique to the area, there have been mines in Wyoming and Montana for nearly 150 years. The mining company had received awards for being environmentally responsible and safe. The mine was on Private Property three miles from the nearest border of the Park. The company had met all the requirements of the U.S. Forest Service and U.S. Environmental Protection Agency making sure that all necessary precautions were being taken to ensure they would be environmentally responsible.

None of this mattered to the UNESCO Heritage Committee who considered the project a potential threat. At the time, there were NO American Representatives on the committee. UNESCO forced the mining company to abandon the project violating the company's private property rights.

The UNESCO did not care that forcing the closure of the mining company's project violated the United States Federal Law prohibiting the inclusion of non-federal property within a U.S. World Heritage Site without the consent of the property owner. The mining company did as they were told and shut down the project and lost millions of dollars in revenue. The closure of the project also cost the community about 300 jobs. But none of this mattered to UNESCO.

I'm waiting for the day UNESCO exerts its legal right to all of us, as American citizens, barring us from being able to visit our own National landmarks and treasures. Since most environmentalists believe the presence of humans disturbs the environment and the ecology, it is not too farfetched that Politically Correct UNESCO will ban the American public from Yellowstone, Yosemite, the Everglades, or the Grand Canyon. Everglades National Park was added to the World Heritage Site in Danger list in 2010 and has, as of the time I was writing this, not been removed. Are you ready to accept that?

I believe our historical landmarks, great works of art, National parks and cultural sites should be protected and maybe UNESCO should be allowed to monitor those areas to insure they are protected. But UNESCO should not have the sole authority and responsibility for those sites. It should be up to our Forest Service. Isn't that what we pay them for.

Solution:

There a couple of solutions.

1. Nations back out of treaties all the time. We need to back out of this World Heritage Treaty and give our historical sites and landmarks back to the American people.

2. Allow UNESCO to monitor the sites, however, the control of visitation and restrictions rest wholly on the host nation. If UNESCO identifies a problem, they notify the host nation and the host nation takes necessary action.

POLITICALLY INCORRECT

I felt compelled to write this chapter because of the 225-year public outcry that there must be a separation of church and state. Ladies and Gentlemen, we can't have it both ways. Either we separate the two or we don't. We can't pick and choose when to and when not to separate the church from the state.

We have taken prayer and the Pledge of Allegiance out of our schools. We have changed wording on National Monuments to omit the word "God." We have changed the names of School Mascots, Sports Teams, and roads because we might offend some individual or group. We've rewritten the history books in our schools because someone was offended by the fact that history painted a tainted picture of the Indians during the Indian Wars, or the Nazi and death camps of WWII because they told what happened in history. **WHERE DOES IT STOP?**

Abraham Lincoln said it best: "You can please some of the people all of the time and all of the people some of the time, but you cannot please all of the people all of the time." It is time to stop trying to please all of the people all of the time!

This Country was founded on the principles of "God." Regardless of religious preference, most have some type of "God" or higher Deity, except for Atheists and I've yet to hear of an atheist group lobbying to remove "God" from anything in the United States. The motto of this Country is "In God We Trust." It's on our currency, in the Great Seal of the President and contained in every document that established the United States of America. Yet, now it's political incorrect to publicly use the term "God" except on the signs of our churches. If we keep bending to be politically correct soon it will be against the law for "the Church of God" to have any sign that displays their name to public view.

Our National Language has been English for over two centuries. It was not changed when immigrants were coming to America to settle this country. When California, Nevada, Arizona, New Mexico and Texas were territories, the population was predominately Spanish and Mexican. For them to become States, they had to accept English as their language. They did. Yet today, we make concessions and laws that require instructions and labeling to contain multiple languages. I recently purchased two appliances. One was manufactured in the United States (Surprised? I was). The other was manufactured in Vietnam. The operator's manual for the American made unit was half an inch thick because it contained instruction in no less than eight different languages, including English, Chinese, Japanese, Arabic, Russian, German, French and Spanish. I can understand this if the appliance is being exported to these various countries, since the instructions would need to be in a language common to the country of purchase, but how many trees could we save by only putting those languages in the cartons being exported. The Vietnamese unit on the other hand had no owner's manual. at all in the packaging. It had a website address where you could find the owner's manual in whatever language you want and print it, saving thousands of trees.

Here are a couple of issues that Government should avoid all together:

1.) Abortion and Gay Marriage. These are church and religious issues with which our Government has no business being involved. These are issues of personal religious and moral conscience. These subjects are forefront of every election and every candidate debate and our representatives spend more time, money and energy arguing over these issues than any other issue before Congress. Government is not in the business of dictating moral convictions, it's in the business of protecting the rights of all people. Separate church and state. You can't ask for separation then turn around and ask the state to rule on a church issue.

2.) School Prayer. I personally believe that if we can allow Muslims to perform their many daily prayer times in the schools then we need to put multi-denominational prayer time back into the schools for everyone.

3.) The Pledge of Allegiance. I also believe the Pledge of Allegiance should be reintroduced as a first activity of the morning. We shouldn't need to reword the praise "under God" because it does not pledge to "God" it's a pledge of loyalty to the Country which is **"One Nation"** under God. Maybe if more of our young people were to understand the Pledge of Allegiance and what it means and represents, they would be better citizens. It is an Oath of Faithfulness to the Country they live in and supports them.

"I pledge allegiance to the Flag of the United States of America, and to the Republic for which it stands, one Nation under God, indivisible, with liberty and justice for all."

RUMORS, MYTHS, LIES AND MISCONCEPTIONS

As I said in the Forward, I think it is important to correct the rumors, lies and misconceptions found on the internet, in emails, from friends, from relatives, and from anti-government sources about our Government. As I have shown, our Government is quite good at causing its own problems without any outside help. I have laid out the facts here and hope that in the future you will simply delete these as spam and not forward them and keep them circulating year after year.

Rumor: Our Representatives can draw a full retirement after serving only one 2-year term of office.

False: Our Representatives do not and cannot draw a full salary retirement after only serving a two-year term. They are bound by the retirement regulations of the Office of Personnel Management, OPM.

Every Company or Business in the United States has some type of retirement plan. Even Government and Civil Service have an extensive retirement plan. Most private sector retirement plans require that an employee serve the company for a minimum of 20 years or until mandatory retirement age, 62 or 65 years of age. OPM requires that any Federal employee, including our Representatives, born after 1964 must meet a minimum retirement age of 57 years old and have at least 10 years Federal Service. Our Representatives must meet the criteria outlined in the OPM regulations. Representatives have the option of contributing to the Federal Retirement System (FERS) and are vested after serving for five years. Vested means that, if after serving for five years they leave office before reaching the OPM minimum retirement requirement, they can withdraw their retirement contributions plus the matching dollar amount, but they can only make this withdrawal if they are 62 years old or older. If they leave office before they are eligible for retirement they can either withdraw their contributed funds or leave those FERS invested funds drawing interest and draw until they reach minimum retirement age or 62 years old. The retirement pension for Representatives who take this last option is around $39,000 to $45,000 per year. If they are in office long enough to meet the minimum FERS retirement age requirement for eligibility, they will receive between one third to one half of their annual salary depending on years of service. As of 2014, a few Senior Representatives with 32 years of service were receiving pension payments of about $139,000 per year.

Rumor: The Families of our elected officials as well as the Families of Staffers of our Representatives do not have to repay their Student Loans.

False: If they have student loans they are required just like everyone else to repay those loans. This rumor is a misconception of a bill that was passed allowing various Government Departments and Agencies to repay Student Loans as a recruiting tool to get professionals to seek employment with the government. There is a need for professionals in many of the different departments of our Government and these professionals are necessary, i.e. Doctors and Nurses for Veterans Administration (VA) and Military hospitals, Lawyers for the Department of Justice and Accountants for the Treasury just to name a few. Businesses throughout the country use this type of recruiting as an enticement to graduating college students to seek employment with their businesses, agencies or organizations.

Rumor: President Obama has written more Executive Orders than any other president.

False: As of November 2014, President Obama had written 194 Executive Orders during his first six years of office. This is a long way from the 3,522 orders written by President Franklin D. Roosevelt. In fact, most of the Presidents since Abraham Lincoln have averaged about 150 orders per term and President Obama was not the first President to have an Executive Order challenged by Congress, Senate, or the Supreme Court. It is true however that President Obama has written more controversial Executive Orders than most Presidents. And during 2010 The States sued the Federal Government a record 52 times.

Rumor: Our Representatives are exempt from paying Taxes and Social Security?

False: Our Representatives must file taxes just like everyone else, but, as with most people with a mass of wealth, their accountants will search out and use any exemption they can to reduce the tax burden. Thus, most representatives pay far less income tax than the people they represent. This is another point that reinforces the repeal of the 16th Amendment or impose a flat tax with no exemptions for all people regardless of income, class or status. As for Social Security, all our elected officials and other Federal employees pay into Social Security. Under the old Federal Retirement System, Civil Service Retirement System (CSRS), Federal employees were exempted from paying Social Security, however they were also exempt from being able to draw Social Security after reaching Retirement Age. Under the new system, Federal Employees Retirement System (FERS), Federal Employees are required to pay Social Security and may draw Social Security entitlements upon reaching Retirement Age. Remember that Social Security is a regressive tax, the more you make the less you pay.

Rumor: Our Representatives have exempted themselves from prosecution for sexual harassment and many other laws they have passed and under which ordinary citizens must live.

False: This is a very blatant lie about our government. Sexual Harassment is a crime and one that OPM and the Government take extremely seriously. Anyone suspected of Sexual Harassment is censured until a formal investigation is conducted and then if found guilty they are removed from their position. Any Government employee, regardless of position, found guilty of Sexual Harassment is subject to immediate dismissal and possible criminal charges depending on the nature and degree of the offense. Although, there are a few laws that don't seem to affect our Representatives, Sexual Harassment is not one of them and I have addressed many of the others throughout this book.

The latest grouping of rumors, lies and misconceptions circulating on the internet concern Patient Protection and Affordable Care Act (Obamacare).

Rumor: Our Representatives have exempted themselves from the Patient Protection and Affordable Care Act (Obamacare).

This is True: When I first read this rumor about a month before deciding to write this book and about 10 months after Obamacare went into effect. I was not surprised that Congress would attempt to exclude themselves and frankly, I was angered by what I read. The truth is, our Representatives cannot exempt themselves from this Act. Per OPM, our Representatives as well as all other

Government employees are given a list of several Health Care Providers in a service called an exchange. Government employees choose their health care provider from the available list. This is the same type exchange that many civilian employers use. What is an exchange? An exchange is a group of Insurance providers that agree to provide Group Health Care Coverage to a Company. Since we are talking about the Government we will use their exchange for the example. The Exchange consists of Blue Cross/Blue Shield, Alliance, Postal Workers, and United Health and there are also localized insurance companies available in the exchange. Government employees may choose from any of these providers. Under Obamacare, Representatives and all other government employees must choose a provider from the exchange and pay the appropriate premium for that provider.

This email rumor circulated from the beginning of Obamacare in 2012 until the campaigns of the 2016 election. OPM standing by its statement that the rumor wasn't true. However, Senator Ted Cruz(R) from Texas during a debate of the Iran Arms deal in 2016, blasted the Senate floor and condemned the deal made with President Obama that the Senate and House would pass the health care measure if they would be exempt from having to participate in Obamacare.

Rumor: Persons can opt out of Obamacare without prosecution or penalty.

False: It is a misinterpretation of U.S. Code 18115 which I copied here

"42 U.S. CODE § 18115 - FREEDOM NOT TO PARTICIPATE IN FEDERAL HEALTH INSURANCE PROGRAMS

No individual, company, business, nonprofit entity, or health insurance issuer offering group or individual health insurance coverage shall be required to participate in any Federal health insurance program created under this Act (or any amendments made by this Act), or in any Federal health insurance program expanded by this Act (or any such amendments), and there shall be no penalty or fine imposed upon any such issuer for choosing not to participate in such programs."

Although, the wording is rather mottled and confusing, this Code does not mean the individuals can exempt themselves. It means just what it says, that Insurance <u>providers</u> do not have to participate in the program. The key word is in the first sentence "<u>issuer</u>". The rest of that sentence reinforces that word and meaning "<u>offering</u> group or individual health insurance <u>coverage</u>".

Rumor: Individuals can be exempt from Obamacare for religious reasons.

This is Both True and False: Certain religions can apply for exemption to Obamacare for conscientious objection reasons. If approved they would be exempt from Obamacare, Government has always taken into consideration the Freedom of Religion afforded to us by the Bill of Rights in the Constitution, but as with any religious freedom, exemptions must be applied for and proof must be given to support the Conscientious Objection.

Here is a rather lengthy explanation of the religious exemption with an explanation of what it means:

"RELIGIOUS CONSCIENCE EXEMPTION — Such term shall not include any individual for any month if such individual has in effect an exemption under section 1311(d) (4) (H) of the Patient Protection and Affordable Care Act which certifies that such individual is a member of a recognized religious sect or division thereof described in section 1402(g) (1) and an adherent of established tenets or teachings of such sect or division as described in such section.

For members of religious groups to qualify for this exemption, they would have to be adherents of a religion or sect "described in section 1402(g)(1)" of the Internal Revenue Code, which governs exemptions from the payment of Social Security and Medicare taxes on self-employment income. In general, persons seeking a health insurance exemption must belong to a religion (or sect thereof) which has been in existence since 1951 and has an established history of spurning participation in insurance programs:

(g) Members of certain religious faiths

(1) Exemption

Any individual may file an application (in such form and manner, and with such official, as may be prescribed by regulations under this chapter) for an exemption from the tax imposed by this chapter if he is a member of a recognized religious sect or division thereof and is an adherent of established tenets or teachings of such sect or division by reason of which he is conscientiously opposed to acceptance of the benefits of any private or public insurance which makes payments in the event of death, disability, old-age, or retirement or makes payments toward the cost of, or provides services for, medical care (including the benefits of any insurance system established by the Social Security Act). Such exemption may be granted only if the application contains or is accompanied by -

(A) such evidence of such individual's membership in, and adherence to the tenets or teachings of, the sect or division thereof as the Secretary may require for purposes of determining such individual's compliance with the preceding sentence, and

(B) his waiver of all benefits and other payments under titles II and XVIII of the Social Security Act based on his wages and self-employment income as well as all such benefits and other payments to him based on the wages and self-employment income of any other person, and only if the Commissioner of Social Security finds that -

(C) Such sect or division thereof has the established tenets or teachings referred to in the preceding sentence,

(D) it is the practice, and has been for a period of time which he deems to be substantial, for members of such sect or division thereof to make provision for their dependent members which in his judgment is reasonable in view of their general level of living, and

(E) Such sect or division thereof has been in existence at all times since December 31, 1950.

An exemption may not be granted to any individual if any benefit or other payment referred to in subparagraph (B) became payable (or, but for section 203 or 222(b) of the Social Security Act, would have become payable) at or before the time of the filing of such waiver."

Basically, what this is saying is, any individual can apply for exemption, but they must prove they are devout followers of their religion and their religion has a history of shunning insurance of any kind. This history of no insurance of any kind makes approval of the application very difficult.

It is interesting that the application for exemption must be made to the IRS. President Obama and Congress have repeatedly told us that Obamacare won't be a tax. If it isn't a tax, wouldn't the application be under the cognizance of the Department of Health, Education and Welfare?

GOVERNMENT'S INTERNATIONAL BLUNDERS?

This chapter is mostly speculative. There are few or no documents available to prove or dispute some of the information provided here. The circumstances surrounding many of these events give way to the fact that our Government may have been covertly involved through use of the Central Intelligence Agency (CIA).

Many believe the American paranoia about Communism began after World War II when there was a strong anti-communist movement in the U.S. The slogan was "Better Dead, Than Red". In reality, it began in 1917. The "First Red Scare" was a result of the Communist/Socialist Party's emergence as a recognized political force with a membership of approximately 75,000 by 1930. It was during this period that political groups like the John Birch Society gained strength. The "Second Red Scare" originated when President Truman issued an Executive Order in 1947 requiring all Federal Civil Service employees to be screened for loyalty. The criteria for determining loyalty was searching for affiliations with any group or organization deemed by the Attorney General to be subversive, totalitarian, Communist or Fascist.

Although Senator Joseph McCarthy was not formally involved until 1950, the period 1917-1956 became known as the McCarthy Era. Senator McCarthy gave speeches, held hearings and conducted investigations of government employees, the entertainment industry and unions. Those who were accused of any association with these groups were harassed and/or terminated even if the accusations couldn't be proven. Some were viciously attacked or imprisoned. Many lost their employment and had shattered careers. A few were executed.

Throughout the 60s and 70s the "Better Dead, Than Red"

sentiment in Washington, D.C. was still very strong and our Government became active in both overt (not hidden) and covert (clandestine or hidden) operations in many different countries to stop the "Red Wave". The Korean War (Police Action) was one such overt operation.

Another overt operation happened in 1960. President Eisenhower was concerned with the ties Fidel Castro of Cuba was forging with the Soviet Union. Congress allocated 13.1 million dollars to the CIA to plan an invasion to overthrow Castro. The CIA recruited and trained exiled Cuban refugees and mercenaries, code named Brigade 2506, to perform the invasion and was supposed to be supported by the U.S. Navy and Air Force. When Kennedy won the Presidential election in 1960, the mission was postponed until after President Kennedy took office. Kennedy approved the mission on 4 April 1961 and the CIA launched the invasion on 17 April 1961. This was the infamous "Bay of Pigs" failure. There were several areas which caused the mission's failure. The Naval support was removed because of funding issues.

The Air Force only allocated eight B-26 bombers to support the invasion, four of which were shot down. Brigade 2506's strength was approximately 1500 personnel. The Cuban forces numbered 234,000 personnel. Without the Naval artillery support and stronger air support the mission was doomed to fail by sheer numbers.

Vietnam was another example of Overt intervention into another country's politics. Many believe the Vietnam war was from roughly 1965 until 1975, when in fact the U.S. involvement in Vietnam started in 1955 - ten years earlier than our government told us. This was the longest military conflict in the history of the United States, lasting 19 years, 5 months, 4 weeks and a day. Even before 1955, during World War II, the United States provided arms and training to the Viet Minh, then a coalition of communist and nationalists fighting against control of the Japanese. President Roosevelt and General Stilwell making it abundantly clear that the French would not reacquire control over French Indochina.

The French ceded a loss of parts of Indochina in the southern regions of China to the Chinese leader Chiang Kai-Shek. Battles raged between the French and the Viet Minh leader Ho Chi Minh. In 1954, the Viet Minh won a decisive victory over the French at the Battle of Dien Bien Phu

Both Ho Chi Minh and his leading General, Vo Nguyen Giap received training on tactics and leadership at the U. S. Command and

War College in Quantico, Va. during the 1940s.

In 1954, the Geneva Convention divided North and South Vietnam at the 17th Parallel. Approximately one million minority Catholics and refugees fled the communist Viet Minh controlled North with the aid of the U.S. Seventh Fleet and as many as two million more would have fled if they had not been stopped by the Viet Minh. The relocation was funded by our Government in the amount of 93 million dollars. In the South, approximately 130,000 Revolutionary Regroupees moved North expecting to return to the south in no more than 2 years. The Viet Minh left roughly five to ten thousand cadre in the south as a politico-military sub-structure with the intent of reclaiming the south. These Cadre became leaders of the Viet Cong and they recruited many disgruntled young South Vietnamese into their ranks and trained them in guerilla warfare.

The intent of the Geneva convention was to allow the people to hold elections to decide upon a unified Government. Ho Chi Minh and the Viet Minh wanted a communist government backed by China and the Soviet Union, while Ngo Dinh Diem, wanted a Democratic Republic backed by the Western Alliance, the U.S., Canada, Britain, and Australia. The CIA intervened and influenced the election of Diem who in the words of Vice-President Johnson was the "Winston Churchill of Asia" "The only boy we got out there". Johnson promised Diem more aid in molding a fighting force capable of defeating the communists. President Kennedy, however, believed Diem and the South Vietnamese had to ultimately defeat the North and the guerillas on their own.

Regardless of the number of military advisors or degree of training given to the Army of the Republic of Vietnam (ARVN) they did not improve. Political promotions and corruption, poor leadership, and infiltration by the Viet Cong weakened the ARVN. Two coup attempts on Diem led him to be paranoid and he became more concerned with having a military to defend against a coup rather than the guerillas. Diem was informed by his predominately Catholic advisors that the Buddhists were behind the coup attempts. Diem ordered Colonel Le Quang Tung to raid Buddhist Pagodas. This action caused widespread damage and destruction leaving hundreds of people dead.

In 1962, the U.S. Advisors began the Strategic Hamlet Program. This program was a joint U.S.-South Vietnamese attempt to resettle the rural villages into fortified camps. Thousands of rural

Vietnamese were forced into internment, segregation, and relocation for their protection. This program waned throughout most of 1963 and was terminated in 1964. The only thing the program can claim was it sent even more young Vietnamese to the Viet Cong.

By 1963, the U.S. had 16,000 advisors in Vietnam imbedded in every level of South Vietnam's Military. The U.S. also had a total lack of confidence in Diem. The Majority Buddhists were protesting the prejudicial influence of the wealthier minority Catholics. The State Department and CIA supported the overthrow of Diem; however, no one expected that he would be murdered in the process. One coup after another left South Vietnam in a state of confusion and chaos. Ho Chi Minh took advantage of the chaos by ordering and funding more guerilla activity by the Viet Cong.

From 1961 until the conflict ended in 1975, the CIA ran covert operations out of Cambodia and Laos with Hmong tribesmen. The CIA trained these Hmong to search out and destroy Pathet Lao forces supporting North Vietnam. The CIA also ran operations such as the Phoenix Program and Special Operations Group, Black Ops which performed search and destroy missions against anyone suspected of being Viet Cong. The name was changed to Military Assistance Command, Vietnam, - Studies and Observations Group (MAC-V SOG) to cover what they were really doing. MAC-V was the title for the Military Command in Vietnam and it was in command of all units operating in the country. MAC-V SOG was never a part of MAC-V. The name was simply a cover in case anyone (reporters or investigators) was investigating CIA activity. SOG consisted of CIA operatives, Australian Intelligence, U.S. Army Intelligence, U.S. Special Operations and a collection of MAC-V units and special forces personnel. With emphasis on "special", these personnel had certain training, talents and abilities which made them desirable for CIA purposes.

The rest of the Vietnam conflict is pretty much history, if you can find anywhere to read it accurately. Kennedy was assassinated. Johnson became President and escalated the war. Fifty-eight thousand American men and women died, 304,000 were wounded, not counting those who died later from their wounds, or were wounded in protests inside our country or Veterans who committed suicide due to PTSD.

Our Government and CIA has been involved in covert political operations around the world. Many of these events fall under the heading of "Plausible Deniability", meaning the Government will deny ever having any involvement.

From 1969 through 1979, many Middle Eastern countries were engaged in civil war or warring between tribes for leadership of the country.

In 1969, Libya was strongly in favor of becoming allied with the Soviet Union. The U.S. didn't want that alliance to happen. Muammar Gaddafi was gaining support for leadership and unification of Libya. Our Government felt that if we provided support and arms to Gaddafi we could win him over to ally with the United States instead of the Soviet Union. Through the CIA, we boosted Gaddafi into power. The plan to win him to democracy backfired. Gaddafi became a Soviet backed dictator and although he didn't trust the Soviets, he disliked the west and the United States even more. After many U.N. sanctions for cruelty and violence against Israel and the people of Libya, a U.N. backed Civil War began in February 2011 resulting in the Death of Gaddafi and two of his sons and the imprisonment of Gaddafi's other two sons.

Hafez Al Assad was the leader of Syria from 1971-2000. He, like many in the Middle East, came to power through a series of coups. There is mixed evidence that the U.S. and Soviet Union backed the many coups leading to Assad's presidency, but no direct evidence to suggest it was the U.S. which finally placed him in power.

Idi Amin was the president of Uganda from 1971-1979. The CIA supported Amin's rise to power by supplying bombs and other military equipment to his Army. Amin also received support of arms and money from Israel. By 1975, Amin had rejected the United States and Israel and gained support from Libya's Gaddafi, East Germany and the Soviet Union. In 1979, the U.N. sanctioned Amin and supported the Uganda-Tanzania war, overthrowing Amin's government and sending him into exile.

Osama Bin Laden was the rebel leader of the Al Qaeda in Afghanistan. In 1979, Bin Laden funneled arms, money and fighters from Arab countries into Afghanistan gaining popularity and support of both the Arab nations and Afghan people. Many of the guns and much of the money was provided through CIA sources in the Middle East to help the Afghans defeat the Soviet Union. In 1988, Bin Laden formed the Al Qaeda in Saudi Arabia. In 1992, the Saudi Government banished him and he relocated to the Sudan until U.S. pressure forced him to return to Afghanistan. By 1996, Bin Laden had established a new base of operation and declared war against the United States and in the following years planned and carried out several terrorist attacks against U.S. targets including the 9/11/2001 attack on the World Trade Center and other targets in the United States.

Manuel Noriega was the President of Panama from 1983-1989. From the early 1950s until shortly before he was removed from office, Noriega worked closely with the CIA and was considered one of the most valuable intelligence assets they had in Central America. Noriega also served as a conduit for illegal weapons and equipment for U.S. backed counter-insurgency operations throughout Central and South America. Noriega was a General in the Panamanian Army and through the late 70s worked with the CIA to influence elections and eventually give Noriega the presidency in 1983. Noriega was also a major cocaine trafficker and although the CIA knew this they continued to back him. In 1989, U.S. Forces invaded Panama and arrested Noriega. He was charged with several counts of drug trafficking, racketeering and money laundering. Noriega was sentenced to serve 40 years for crimes against the United States. He was also tried and convicted in France and Panama. He is currently in prison in Panama serving a 20-year sentence that was imposed in 2011.

The Leaders of these additional countries may have also been influenced or assisted covertly by the U. S. Government: Argentina, Bolivia, San Salvador, Guatemala, El Salvador, the Congo and the list goes on. All, in turmoil during the late 1960s and early 1970s. All, having one leader emerge as the supreme one ruler of the country during this period. All, previously had many ruler factions fighting for control and coups which changed the ruler roughly every two years, some even more frequently.

IRAN-CONTRA VS IRAN ARMS DEAL

The Iran-Contra affair or Iran-Contra scandal was a covert arm deal between Iran and the United States between 1987 and 1990. Several senior officials of the Reagan administration secretly negotiated a sale of arms to Iran. At the time the U.S. had an embargo of any trade with Iran. Seven U.S. citizens were being held hostage in Lebanon by a paramilitary group tied to Iran. The officials involved hoped to get these hostages released as well as fund support to the Contra Guerillas in Nicaragua. Congress had prohibited any support to the Contras, indicating the U.S. shouldn't be involved.

The plan was to ship arms through Israel into Iran and the United States would resupply Israel and receive payment for the weapons from Israel. USMC, Colonel Oliver North allegedly modified the plan in late 1985. Part of the sale proceeds were to be diverted to fund the anti-Sandinista rebels or Contras in Nicaragua. Between 1987 and 1990, several of those involved were indicted and prosecuted, however the Officials involved were later pardoned by President Bush. Colonel North was indicted and convicted in 1990, however, in his appeal the charges were dismissed. My belief is that Colonel North was simply a pawn in a high stakes game created by some ranking officials in the Administration. Colonel North did his job as a Marine Officer and followed orders.

The Iran Arms Deal of August 2016. This deal was also a violation of the sanctions banning U.S. dollars from being used in any transaction with Iran. To get past the sanctions, our Government used the Global Banking system to procure 1.7 Billion dollars from Swiss and Netherlands banks then send the foreign currency to Iran. Government Officials said the funds were in payment of contracts owed to Iran since the fall of the Shah in 1979. Oddly enough, the settlement of these contracts after nearly 40 years also procured the release of several American citizens held hostage by Iran. It appeared

Our Government was paying a ransom for the return of the hostages, however, this was denied by the members of Congress and Senate who approved the deal. Why would our Government be reopening a 40-year old arms deal with Iran if for any other reason than to hide the truth from the public?

The difference between the Iran-Contra Scandal and the Iran Arms Deal is basically this; Iran-Contra was a covert operation which was discovered and its perpetrators prosecuted. They may not have served the sentences, but they were tried for the crimes. The Iran Arms Deal was not covert. It was published and addressed by the White House and Congress in the media. The fact that **we, the people,** were being lied to and deceived, makes the deal equally as illegal as the Iran-Contra. The Government members who perpetrated this illegal activity should be prosecuted. **The Iran Arms Deal is just a Contra deal in new clothing.** It is still ransom for hostages.

WHAT IS THE PLAN FOR THE UNITED STATES?

There are as many forms of Government as there are and have been countries in the world. From Empires, Monarchies and Dictatorships to Capitalist, Socialist and Communist, we have seen them all. Kings, Emirates, Pashas, Emperors, Czars, Dictators and Presidents, the Senators of the Roman Empire to the Congress of the United States they are all the same. Once empowered, they seem to forget it is the people make them who they are. Without the people, there is no Country and without the country there is no need for government.

There are three of these types of Government that concern us here in the United States. Capitalist, which is how we've believed for most of our history. Communist, which we have been fighting against for most of the past seventy years and Socialist, which many believe is the same as Communist. Although the two types are very close, they are not the same. Communism is more of an offspring, a result of, and a child born of Socialism.

Here are some definitions that might be helpful.

Merriam-Webster's Dictionary provides the following definitions:

Capitalism:

An economic system characterized by
private or corporation ownership of capital goods and by prices, production and distribution of goods that are determined by a free market.

Capitalist:
A person who has capital invested in a business

A person of great wealth

Socialism:
>*A theory of Social Organization based on Government ownership, management and control of the means of production and distribution and exchange of goods.*

Socialist:
>*A person who believes in and practices Socialism.*

Communism:
>*Social Organization in which goods are held in common.*
>*A theory of Social Organization advocating common ownership, management and control of the means of production and distribution of products of industry based on need.*

Communist:
>*A person who believes in and practices communism.*

You can see that these three types of Government are very different. Capitalism is private ownership. Socialism is Government ownership and Communism is communal ownership.

I define these types of Government because of the direction our Country is heading. At the end of World War II the United States was a Capitalist nation. Our biggest adversaries were Russia, a socialist country and China, a communist country, but of course we all know this. Think of the world in terms of the big blue marble it is with socialist Russia, the United Soviet Socialist Republic (USSR) and communist China on one side and capitalist USA on the other, this is how the world looked in 1945. Over the next fifty years the axis of the marble shifted slowly. The USA became gradually more Socialist and the USSR became gradually more Capitalist. Of course, neither country's Government will admit to these changes. However, the proof is in the pudding so to speak. The U. S. Government has introduced more bills and laws giving more control to Government and created more programs to make its population dependent on Government while the USSR dissolved and Russia invested more to gain capital wealth. Communist China, gained both on the capitalist side and the socialist side, The Government controls everything from the socialist view but the people all work together for the greater good of the country from the communist view. The countries of Denmark, Belgium, Norway and Sweden have about the strongest currency and best governing practices. They are all Constitutional Monarchies much like England and democratic like the U.S. with one exception. The parties of their Parliaments work together for the greater good of the people and the country. Their parties don't vie for power over one another and don't try to control the people. The people of these countries work together for the betterment of the country. Their welfare is a supplement to the wages earned, not just a handout from the government. They must work to receive the benefit. Their Social Security for the elderly takes care of medical, housing and money they can live on.

Every form of government has some issues and the grass is always greener somewhere else, but without the population and government working together, Governments fall and we either have a revolution or some other country comes in to take over. Capitalism and Socialism have been around for ages. Capitalistic Countries have failed because their leadership wanted more and more power and control so the capitalist gave way to the socialist. History has repeatedly shown the rise of countries like Ancient Greece, Prussia, and the Roman Empire and starting out as Militarily Majestic Empires which formed Democratic Republics, transitioned to Socialism to maintain control over their populations and ultimately collapsed. Socialism or socialist policies have failed in just about every country which leans toward them. Socialism removes the will to work from the population and those who do the work are giving away their labor to those who don't. Eventually, the country has no national product because it has no part of the population which is will to work. The country must outsource everything to other countries. In 1989, we saw the value of the Russian Ruble at an all-time low, the oil market prices, which the Soviet Union had relied so heavily, crashed. This left the Soviets without any other product which they could export to maintain the solvency of their currency. As we know the USSR began to lose control over the "satellite" countries, like Ukraine, Georgia and Latvia and eventually the entire Soviet Union failed.

Where is the United States in all of this? What is the Governments plan for the Country? Can we fix what's broken and make our country better? You tell me. All I can say is that if we all work together we can make a better plan and a better country.

IN CONCLUSION

The problem with writing a definitive book on our Government is that every day the newspapers report more and more evidence of the abuses, stupidity and corruption. Senators and Congresspersons resign before being tried and convicted of crimes against the people they represent. Blackmail between members of different offices and tit for tat (I'll back your bill if you back mine) representation. Charges of bribery, pandering, accepting bribes and embezzlement. Where does it end? I had to pick a stopping point or this book would never have been completed.

The other problem with writing a book on Government is being careful to not alienate the readers. I know this book will offend some people and enlighten others. Some will feel it is just regurgitation of what we hear in the news. I said from the beginning there isn't anything here that hasn't been said before. Now it is all in one place with some ideas for solutions.

Hopefully, I have identified and offered solutions to some of the problems with our Government. I could go much deeper into a few of those problems as well as show you where our Government has been planning and working to dictate how we think and act. This work is an effort to right the wrongs of our government and get them back on track to be a Government, OF, BY and FOR the People.

THE CONSTITUTION
OF THE
UNITED STATES OF AMERICA

PREAMBLE

We the People of the United States, in Order to form a more perfect Union, establish Justice, insure domestic Tranquility, provide for the common defense, promote the general Welfare, and secure the Blessings of Liberty to ourselves and our Posterity, do ordain and establish this Constitution for the United States of America.

Article. I.

Section. 1.

All legislative Powers herein granted shall be vested in a Congress of the United States, which shall consist of a Senate and House of Representatives.

Section. 2.

The House of Representatives shall be composed of Members chosen every second Year by the People of the several States, and the Electors in each State shall have the Qualifications requisite for Electors of the most numerous Branch of the State Legislature.

No Person shall be a Representative who shall not have attained to the Age of twenty-five Years, and been seven Years a Citizen of the United States, and who shall not, when elected, be an Inhabitant of that State in which he shall be chosen.

Representatives and direct Taxes shall be apportioned among the several States which may be included within this Union, according to their respective Numbers, which shall be determined by adding to the whole Number of free Persons, including those bound to Service for a Term of Years, and excluding Indians not taxed, three fifths of all other Persons. The actual Enumeration shall be made within three Years after the first Meeting of the Congress of the United States, and within every subsequent Term of ten Years, in such Manner as they shall by Law direct. The Number of Representatives shall not exceed one for every thirty Thousand, but each State shall have at Least one Representative; and until such enumeration shall be made, the State of New Hampshire shall be entitled to choose three, Massachusetts eight, Rhode-Island and Providence Plantations one, Connecticut five, New-York six, New Jersey four, Pennsylvania eight, Delaware one, Maryland six, Virginia ten, North Carolina five, South Carolina five, and Georgia three.

When vacancies happen in the Representation from any State, the Executive Authority thereof shall issue Writs of Election to fill such Vacancies.

The House of Representatives shall chose their Speaker and other Officers; and shall have the sole Power of Impeachment.

Section. 3.

The Senate of the United States shall be composed of two Senators from each State, chosen by the Legislature thereof, for six Years; and each Senator shall have one Vote.
Immediately after they shall be assembled in Consequence of the first Election, they shall be divided as equally as may be into three Classes. The Seats of the Senators of the first Class shall be vacated at the Expiration of the second Year, of the second Class at the Expiration of the fourth Year, and of the third Class at the Expiration of the sixth Year, so that one third may be chosen every second Year; and if Vacancies happen by Resignation, or otherwise, during the Recess of the Legislature of any State, the Executive thereof may make temporary Appointments until the next Meeting of the Legislature, which shall then fill such Vacancies.

No Person shall be a Senator who shall not have attained to the Age of thirty Years, and been nine Years a Citizen of the United States, and who shall not, when elected, be an Inhabitant of that State for which he shall be chosen.

The Vice President of the United States shall be President of the Senate, but shall have no Vote, unless they be equally divided.

The Senate shall chose their other Officers, and also a President pro tempore, in the Absence of the Vice President, or when he shall exercise the Office of President of the United States.

The Senate shall have the sole Power to try all Impeachments. When sitting for that Purpose, they shall be on Oath or Affirmation. When the President of the United States is tried, the Chief Justice shall preside: And no Person shall be convicted without the Concurrence of two thirds of the Members present.

Judgment in Cases of Impeachment shall not extend further than to removal from Office, and disqualification to hold and enjoy any Office of honor, Trust or Profit under the United States: but the Party convicted shall nevertheless be liable and subject to Indictment, Trial, Judgment and Punishment, according to Law.

Section. 4.

The Times, Places and Manner of holding Elections for Senators and Representatives, shall be prescribed in each State by the Legislature thereof; but the Congress may at any time by Law make or alter such Regulations, except as to the Places of choosing Senators.

The Congress shall assemble at least once in every Year, and such Meeting shall be on the first Monday in December, unless they shall by Law appoint a different Day.

Section. 5.

Each House shall be the Judge of the Elections, Returns and Qualifications of its own Members, and a Majority of each shall constitute a Quorum to do Business; but a smaller number may adjourn from day to day, and may be authorized to compel the Attendance of absent Members, in such Manner, and under such Penalties as each House may provide.

Each House may determine the Rules of its Proceedings, punish its Members for disorderly Behavior, and, with the Concurrence of two thirds, expel a Member.

Each House shall keep a Journal of its Proceedings, and from time to time publish the same, excepting such Parts as May in their Judgment require Secrecy; and the Yeas and Nays of the Members of either House on any question shall, at the Desire of one fifth of those Present, be entered on the Journal.

Neither House, during the Session of Congress, shall, without the Consent of the other, adjourn for more than three days, nor to any other Place than that in which the two Houses shall be sitting.

Section. 6.

The Senators and Representatives shall receive a Compensation for their Services, to be ascertained by Law, and paid out of the Treasury of the United States. They shall in all Cases, except Treason, Felony and Breach of the Peace, be privileged from Arrest during their attendance at the Session of their respective

Houses, and in going to and returning from the same; and for any Speech or Debate in either House, they shall not be questioned in any other Place.

No Senator or Representative shall, during the Time for which he was elected, be appointed to any civil Office under the Authority of the United States, which shall have been created, or the Emoluments whereof shall have been increased during such time; and no Person holding any Office under the United States, shall be a Member of either House during his Continuance in Office.

Section. 7.

All Bills for raising Revenue shall originate in the House of Representatives; but the Senate may propose or concur with Amendments as on other Bills.

Every Bill which shall have passed the House of Representatives and the Senate, shall, before it become a Law, be presented to the President of the United States; If he approve he shall sign it, but if not he shall return it, with his Objections to that House in which it shall have originated, who shall enter the Objections at large on their Journal, and proceed to reconsider it. If after such Reconsideration two thirds of that House shall agree to pass the Bill, it shall be sent, together with the Objections, to the other House, by which it shall likewise be reconsidered, and if approved by two thirds of that House, it shall become a Law. But in all such Cases the Votes of both Houses shall be determined by yeas and Nays, and the Names of the Persons voting for and against the Bill shall be entered on the Journal of each House respectively. If any Bill shall not be returned by the President within ten Days (Sundays excepted) after it shall have been presented to him, the same shall be a Law, in like Manner as if he had signed it, unless the Congress by their Adjournment prevent its Return, in which Case it shall not be a Law.

Every Order, Resolution, or Vote to which the Concurrence of the Senate and House of Representatives may be necessary (except on a question of Adjournment) shall be presented to the President of the United States; and before the Same shall take Effect, shall be approved by him, or being disapproved by him, shall be repassed by two thirds of the Senate and House of Representatives, according to the Rules and Limitations prescribed in the Case of a Bill.

Section. 8.

The Congress shall have Power To lay and collect Taxes,

Duties, Imposts and Excises, to pay the Debts and provide for the common Defense and general Welfare of the United States; but all Duties, Imposts and Excises shall be uniform throughout the United States;

To borrow Money on the credit of the United States;

To regulate Commerce with foreign Nations, and among the several States, and with the Indian Tribes;

To establish an uniform Rule of Naturalization, and uniform Laws on the subject of Bankruptcies throughout the United States;

To coin Money, regulate the Value thereof, and of foreign Coin, and fix the Standard of Weights and Measures;

To provide for the Punishment of counterfeiting the Securities and current Coin of the United States;

To establish Post Offices and post Roads;

To promote the Progress of Science and useful Arts, by securing for limited Times to Authors and Inventors the exclusive Right to their respective Writings and Discoveries;

To constitute Tribunals inferior to the Supreme Court;

To define and punish Piracies and Felonies committed on the high Seas, and Offences against the Law of Nations;

To declare War, grant Letters of Marque and Reprisal, and make Rules concerning Captures on Land and Water;

To raise and support Armies, but no Appropriation of Money to that Use shall be for a longer Term than two Years;

To provide and maintain a Navy;

To make Rules for the Government and Regulation of the land and naval Forces;

To provide for calling forth the Militia to execute the Laws of the Union, suppress Insurrections and repel Invasions;

To provide for organizing, arming, and disciplining, the Militia, and for governing such Part of them as may be employed in the Service of the United States, reserving to the States respectively, the Appointment of the Officers, and the Authority of training the Militia according to the discipline prescribed by Congress;

To exercise exclusive Legislation in all Cases whatsoever, over such District (not exceeding ten Miles square) as may, by Cession of particular States, and the Acceptance of Congress, become the Seat of the Government of the United States, and to exercise like Authority over all Places purchased by the Consent of the Legislature of the State in which the Same shall be, for the Erection of Forts, Magazines, Arsenals, dock-Yards, and other needful Buildings; —

And

To make all Laws which shall be necessary and proper for carrying into Execution the foregoing Powers, and all other Powers vested by this Constitution in the Government of the United States, or in any Department or Officer thereof.

Section. 9.

The Migration or Importation of such Persons as any of the States now existing shall think proper to admit, shall not be prohibited by the Congress prior to the Year one thousand eight hundred and eight, but a Tax or duty may be imposed on such Importation, not exceeding ten dollars for each Person.

The Privilege of the Writ of Habeas Corpus shall not be suspended, unless when in Cases of Rebellion or Invasion the public Safety may require it.

No Bill of Attainder or ex post facto Law shall be passed.

No Capitation, or other direct, Tax shall be laid, unless in Proportion to the Census or enumeration herein before directed to be taken.

No Tax or Duty shall be laid on Articles exported from any State.

No Preference shall be given by any Regulation of Commerce or Revenue to the Ports of one State over those of another: nor shall Vessels bound to, or from, one State, be obliged to enter, clear, or pay Duties in another.

No Money shall be drawn from the Treasury, but in Consequence of Appropriations made by Law; and a regular Statement and Account of the Receipts and Expenditures of all public Money shall be published from time to time.

No Title of Nobility shall be granted by the United States: And no Person holding any Office of Profit or Trust under them, shall, without the Consent of the Congress, accept of any present, Emolument, Office, or Title, of any kind whatever, from any King, Prince, or foreign State.

Section. 10.

No State shall enter into any Treaty, Alliance, or Confederation; grant Letters of Marque and Reprisal; coin Money; emit Bills of Credit; make any Thing but gold and silver Coin a Tender in Payment of Debts; pass any Bill of Attainder, ex post facto Law, or Law impairing the Obligation of Contracts, or grant any Title of Nobility.

No State shall, without the Consent of the Congress, lay any Imposts or Duties on Imports or Exports, except what may be absolutely necessary for executing it's inspection Laws: and the net Produce of all Duties and Imposts, laid by any State on Imports or Exports, shall be for the Use of the Treasury of the United States; and all such Laws shall be subject to the Revision and Control of the Congress.

No State shall, without the Consent of Congress, lay any Duty of Tonnage, keep Troops, or Ships of War in time of Peace, enter into any Agreement or Compact with another State, or with a foreign Power, or engage in War, unless actually invaded, or in such imminent Danger as will not admit of delay.

Article. II.

Section. 1.

The executive Power shall be vested in a President of the United States of America. He shall hold his Office during the Term of four Years, and, together with the Vice President, chosen for the same Term, be elected, as follows

Each State shall appoint, in such Manner as the Legislature thereof may direct, a Number of Electors, equal to the whole Number of Senators and Representatives to which the State may be entitled in the Congress: but no Senator or Representative, or Person holding an Office of Trust or Profit under the United States, shall be appointed an Elector.

The Electors shall meet in their respective States, and vote by Ballot for two Persons, of whom one at least shall not be an Inhabitant of the same State with themselves. And they shall make a List of all the Persons voted for, and of the Number of Votes for each; which List they shall sign and certify, and transmit sealed to the Seat of the Government of the United States, directed to the President of the Senate. The President of the Senate shall, in the Presence of the Senate and House of Representatives, open all the Certificates, and the Votes shall then be counted. The Person having the greatest Number of Votes shall be the President, if such Number be a Majority of the whole Number of Electors appointed; and if there be more than one who have such Majority, and have an equal Number of Votes, then the House of Representatives shall immediately chose by Ballot one of them for President; and if no Person have a Majority, then from the five highest on the List the said House shall in like Manner chose the President. But in choosing the President, the Votes shall be taken by States, the Representation from each State having one Vote; a quorum for this Purpose shall consist of a Member or Members from two thirds of the States, and a Majority of all the States shall be necessary to a Choice. In every Case, after the Choice of the President, the Person having the greatest Number of Votes of the Electors shall be the Vice President. But if there should remain two or more who have equal Votes, the Senate shall chose from them by Ballot the Vice President.

The Congress may determine the Time of choosing the Electors, and the Day on which they shall give their Votes; which Day shall be the same throughout the United States.

No Person except a natural born Citizen, or a Citizen of the United States, at the time of the Adoption of this Constitution, shall be eligible to the Office of President; neither shall any Person be eligible to that Office who shall not have attained to the Age of thirty-five Years, and been fourteen Years a Resident within the United States.

In Case of the Removal of the President from Office, or of his Death, Resignation, or Inability to discharge the Powers and Duties of the said Office, the Same shall devolve on the Vice President, and the Congress may by Law provide for the Case of Removal, Death, Resignation or Inability, both of the President and Vice President, declaring what Officer shall then act as President, and such Officer shall act accordingly, until the Disability be removed, or a President shall be elected.

The President shall, at stated Times, receive for his Services, a Compensation, which shall neither be increased nor diminished during the Period for which he shall have been elected, and he shall not receive within that Period any other Emolument from the United States, or any of them.

Before he enters on the Execution of his Office, he shall take the following Oath or Affirmation: —"I do solemnly swear (or affirm) that I will faithfully execute the Office of President of the United States, and will to the best of my Ability, preserve, protect and defend the Constitution of the United States."

Section. 2.

The President shall be Commander in Chief of the Army and Navy of the United States, and of the Militia of the several States, when called into the actual Service of the United States; he may require the Opinion, in writing, of the principal Officer in each of the executive Departments, upon any Subject relating to the Duties of their respective Offices, and he shall have Power to grant Reprieves and Pardons for Offences against the United States, except in Cases of Impeachment.

He shall have Power, by and with the Advice and Consent of the Senate, to make Treaties, provided two thirds of the Senators present concur; and he shall nominate, and by and with the Advice and Consent of the Senate, shall appoint Ambassadors, other public Ministers and Consuls, Judges of the supreme Court, and all other Officers of the United States, whose Appointments are not herein otherwise provided for, and which shall be established by Law: but the Congress may by Law vest the Appointment of such inferior Officers, as they think proper, in the President alone, in the Courts of Law, or in the Heads of Departments.

The President shall have Power to fill up all Vacancies that may happen during the Recess of the Senate, by granting Commissions which shall expire at the End of their next Session.

Section. 3.

He shall from time to time give to the Congress Information of the State of the Union, and recommend to their Consideration such Measures as he shall judge necessary and expedient; he may, on extraordinary Occasions, convene both Houses, or either of them, and in Case of Disagreement between them, with Respect to the Time of Adjournment, he may adjourn them to such Time as he shall think proper; he shall receive Ambassadors and other public Ministers; he shall take Care that the Laws be faithfully executed, and shall Commission all the Officers of the United States.

Section. 4.

The President, Vice President and all civil Officers of the United States, shall be removed from Office on Impeachment for, and Conviction of, Treason, Bribery, or other high Crimes and Misdemeanors.

Article III.

Section. 1.

The judicial Power of the United States, shall be vested in one

Supreme Court, and in such inferior Courts as the Congress may from time to time ordain and establish. The Judges, both of the supreme and inferior Courts, shall hold their Offices during good Behavior, and shall, at stated Times, receive for their Services, a Compensation, which shall not be diminished during their Continuance in Office.

Section. 2.

The judicial Power shall extend to all Cases, in Law and Equity, arising under this Constitution, the Laws of the United States, and Treaties made, or which shall be made, under their Authority;— to all Cases affecting Ambassadors, other public Ministers and Consuls;—to all Cases of admiralty and maritime Jurisdiction;—to Controversies to which the United States shall be a Party;—to Controversies between two or more States;— between a State and Citizens of another State,—between Citizens of different States,— between Citizens of the same State claiming Lands under Grants of different States, and between a State, or the Citizens thereof, and foreign States, Citizens or Subjects.

In all Cases affecting Ambassadors, other public Ministers and Consuls, and those in which a State shall be Party, the Supreme Court shall have original Jurisdiction. In all the other Cases before mentioned, the Supreme Court shall have appellate Jurisdiction, both as to Law and Fact, with such Exceptions, and under such Regulations as the Congress shall make.

The Trial of all Crimes, except in Cases of Impeachment, shall be by Jury; and such Trial shall be held in the State where the said Crimes shall have been committed; but when not committed within any State, the Trial shall be at such Place or Places as the Congress may by Law have directed.

Section. 3.

Treason against the United States, shall consist only in levying War against them, or in adhering to their Enemies, giving them Aid and Comfort. No Person shall be convicted of Treason unless on the Testimony of two Witnesses to the same overt Act, or on Confession in open Court.

The Congress shall have Power to declare the Punishment of Treason, but no Attainder of Treason shall work Corruption of Blood, or Forfeiture except during the Life of the Person attainted.

Article. IV.

Section. 1.

Full Faith and Credit shall be given in each State to the public Acts, Records, and judicial Proceedings of every other State. And the Congress may by general Laws prescribe the Manner in which such Acts, Records and Proceedings shall be proved, and the Effect thereof.

Section. 2.

The Citizens of each State shall be entitled to all Privileges and Immunities of Citizens in the several States.

A Person charged in any State with Treason, Felony, or other Crime, who shall flee from Justice, and be found in another State, shall on Demand of the executive Authority of the State from which he fled, be delivered up, to be removed to the State having Jurisdiction of the Crime.

No Person held to Service or Labor in one State, under the Laws thereof, escaping into another, shall, in Consequence of any Law or Regulation therein, be discharged from such Service or Labor, but shall be delivered up on Claim of the Party to whom such Service or Labor may be due.

Section. 3.

New States may be admitted by the Congress into this Union; but no new State shall be formed or erected within the Jurisdiction of any other State; nor any State be formed by the Junction of two or more States, or Parts of States, without the Consent of the Legislatures of the States concerned as well as of the Congress.

The Congress shall have Power to dispose of and make all needful Rules and Regulations respecting the Territory or other Property belonging to the United States; and nothing in this Constitution shall be so construed as to Prejudice any Claims of the United States, or of any particular State.

Section. 4.

The United States shall guarantee to every State in this Union a Republican Form of Government, and shall protect each of them against Invasion; and on Application of the Legislature, or of the Executive (when the Legislature cannot be convened), against domestic Violence.

Article. V.

The Congress, whenever two thirds of both Houses shall deem it necessary, shall propose Amendments to this Constitution, or, on the Application of the Legislatures of two thirds of the several States, shall call a Convention for proposing Amendments, which, in either Case, shall be valid to all Intents and Purposes, as Part of this Constitution, when ratified by the Legislatures of three fourths of the several States, or by Conventions in three fourths thereof, as the one or the other Mode of Ratification may be proposed by the Congress; Provided that no Amendment which may be made prior to the Year One thousand eight hundred and eight shall in any Manner affect the first and fourth Clauses in the Ninth Section of the first Article; and that no State, without its Consent, shall be deprived of its equal Suffrage in the Senate.

Article. VI.

All Debts contracted and Engagements entered into, before the Adoption of this Constitution, shall be as valid against the United States under this Constitution, as under the Confederation.

This Constitution, and the Laws of the United States which shall be made in Pursuance thereof; and all Treaties made, or which shall be made, under the Authority of the United States, shall be the supreme Law of the Land; and the Judges in every State shall be bound thereby, any Thing in the Constitution or Laws of any State to the Contrary notwithstanding.

The Senators and Representatives before mentioned, and the Members of the several State Legislatures, and all executive and judicial Officers, both of the United States and of the several States, shall be bound by Oath or Affirmation, to support this Constitution; but no religious Test shall ever be required as a Qualification to any Office or public Trust under the United States.

Article. VII.

The Ratification of the Conventions of nine States, shall be sufficient for the Establishment of this Constitution between the States so ratifying the same.

Amendment I

Congress shall make no law respecting an establishment of religion, or prohibiting the free exercise thereof; or abridging the freedom of speech, or of the press; or the right of the people peaceably to assemble, and to petition the Government for a redress of grievances.

Amendment II

A well-regulated Militia, being necessary to the security of a Free State, the right of the people to keep and bear Arms, shall not be infringed.

Amendment III

No Soldier shall, in time of peace be quartered in any house, without the consent of the Owner, nor in time of war, but in a manner to be prescribed by law.

Amendment IV

The right of the people to be secure in their persons, houses, papers, and effects, against unreasonable searches and seizures, shall not be violated, and no Warrants shall issue, but upon probable cause, supported by Oath or affirmation, and particularly describing the place to be searched, and the persons or things to be seized.

Amendment V

No person shall be held to answer for a capital, or otherwise infamous crime, unless on a presentment or indictment of a Grand Jury, except in cases arising in the land or naval forces, or in the Militia, when in actual service in time of War or public danger; nor shall any person be subject for the same offence to be twice put in jeopardy of life or limb; nor shall be compelled in any criminal case to be a witness against himself, nor be deprived of life, liberty, or property, without due process of law; nor shall private property be taken for public use, without just compensation.

Amendment VI

In all criminal prosecutions, the accused shall enjoy the right to a speedy and public trial, by an impartial jury of the State and district wherein the crime shall have been committed, which district shall have been previously ascertained by law, and to be informed of the nature and cause of the accusation; to be confronted with the witnesses against him; to have compulsory process for obtaining witnesses in his favor, and to have the Assistance of Counsel for his defense.

Amendment VII

In suits at common law, where the value in controversy shall exceed twenty dollars, the right of trial by jury shall be preserved, and no fact tried by a jury, shall be otherwise reexamined in any Court of the United States, than according to the rules of the common law.

Amendment VIII

Excessive bail shall not be required, nor excessive fines imposed, nor cruel and unusual punishments inflicted.

Amendment IX

The enumeration in the Constitution, of certain rights, shall not be construed to deny or disparage others retained by the people.

Amendment X

The powers not delegated to the United States by the Constitution, nor prohibited by it to the States, are reserved to the States respectively, or to the people.

Amendment XI

The Judicial power of the United States shall not be construed to extend to any suit in law or equity, commenced or prosecuted against one of the United States by Citizens of another State, or by Citizens or Subjects of any Foreign State.

Amendment XII

The Electors shall meet in their respective states and vote by ballot for President and Vice-President, one of whom, at least, shall not be an inhabitant of the same state with themselves; they shall name in their ballots the person voted for as President, and in distinct ballots the person voted for as Vice-President, and they shall make distinct lists of all persons voted for as President, and of all persons voted for as Vice-President, and of the number of votes for each, which lists they shall sign and certify, and transmit sealed to the seat of the government of the United States, directed to the President of the Senate; -- The President of the Senate shall, in the presence of the Senate and House of Representatives, open all the certificates and the votes shall then be counted; -- The person having the greatest number of votes for President, shall be the President, if such number be a majority of the whole number of Electors appointed; and if no person have such majority, then from the persons having the highest numbers not exceeding three on the list of those voted for as President, the House of Representatives shall choose immediately, by ballot, the President. But in choosing the President, the votes shall be taken by states, the representation from each state having one vote; a quorum for this purpose shall consist of a member or members from two-thirds of the states, and a majority of all the states shall be necessary to a choice. And if the House of Representatives shall not choose a President whenever the right of choice shall devolve upon them, before the fourth day of March next following, then the Vice-President shall act as President, as in case of the death or other constitutional disability of the President.-- The perso677u8n having the greatest number of votes as Vice-President, shall be the Vice-President, if such number be a majority of the whole number of Electors appointed, and if no person have a majority, then from the two highest numbers on the list, the Senate shall choose the Vice-President; a quorum for the purpose shall consist of two-thirds of the whole number of Senators, and a majority of the whole number shall be necessary to a choice. But no person constitutionally ineligible to the office of President shall be eligible to that of Vice-President of the United States.

Amendment XIII

Section 1.

Neither slavery nor involuntary servitude, except as a punishment for crime whereof the party shall have been duly convicted, shall exist within the United States, or any place subject to their jurisdiction.

Section 2.

Congress shall have power to enforce this article by appropriate legislation.

Amendment XIV

Section 1.

All persons born or naturalized in the United States, and subject to the jurisdiction thereof, are citizens of the United States and of the State wherein they reside. No State shall make or enforce any law which shall abridge the privileges or immunities of citizens of the United States; nor shall any State deprive any person of life, liberty, or property, without due process of law; nor deny to any person within its jurisdiction the equal protection of the laws.

Section 2.

Representatives shall be apportioned among the several States according to their respective numbers, counting the whole number of persons in each State, excluding Indians not taxed. But when the right to vote at any election for the choice of electors for President and Vice-President of the United States, Representatives in Congress, the Executive and Judicial officers of a State, or the members of the Legislature thereof, is denied to any of the male inhabitants of such State, being twenty-one years of age, and citizens of the United States, or in any way abridged, except for participation in rebellion, or other crime, the basis of representation therein shall be reduced in the proportion which the number of such male citizens shall bear to the whole number of male citizens twenty-one years of age in such State.

Section 3.

No person shall be a Senator or Representative in Congress, or elector of President and Vice-President, or hold any office, civil or military, under the United States, or under any State, who, having previously taken an oath, as a member of Congress, or as an officer of the United States, or as a member of any State legislature, or as an executive or judicial officer of any State, to support the Constitution of the United States, shall have engaged in insurrection or rebellion against the same, or given aid or comfort to the enemies thereof. But Congress may by a vote of two-thirds of each House, remove such disability.

Section 4.

The validity of the public debt of the United States, authorized by law, including debts incurred for payment of pensions and bounties for services in suppressing insurrection or rebellion, shall not be questioned. But neither the United States nor any State shall assume or pay any debt or obligation incurred in aid of insurrection or rebellion against the United States, or any claim for the loss or emancipation of any slave; but all such debts, obligations and claims shall be held illegal and void.

Section 5

The Congress shall have the power to enforce, by appropriate legislation, the provisions of this article.

Amendment XV

Section 1.

The right of citizens of the United States to vote shall not be denied or abridged by the United States or by any State on account of race, color, or previous condition of servitude.

Section 2.

The Congress shall have the power to enforce this article by appropriate legislation.

Amendment XVI

The Congress shall have power to lay and collect taxes on incomes, from whatever source derived, without apportionment among the several States, and without regard to any census or enumeration.

Amendment XVII

The Senate of the United States shall be composed of two Senators from each State, elected by the people thereof, for six years; and each Senator shall have one vote. The electors in each State shall have the qualifications requisite for electors of the most numerous branch of the State legislatures.

When vacancies happen in the representation of any State in the Senate, the executive authority of such State shall issue writs of election to fill such vacancies: Provided, that the legislature of any State may empower the executive thereof to make temporary appointments until the people fill the vacancies by election as the legislature may direct.

This amendment shall not be so construed as to affect the election or term of any Senator chosen before it becomes valid as part of the Constitution.

Amendment XVIII

Section 1.

After one year from the ratification of this article the manufacture, sale, or transportation of intoxicating liquors within, the importation thereof into, or the exportation thereof from the United States and all territory subject to the jurisdiction thereof for beverage purposes is hereby prohibited.

Section 2.

The Congress and the several States shall have concurrent power to enforce this article by appropriate legislation.

Section 3.

This article shall be inoperative unless it shall have been ratified as an amendment to the Constitution by the legislatures of the several States, as provided in the Constitution, within seven years from the date of the submission hereof to the States by the Congress.

Amendment XIX

The right of citizens of the United States to vote shall not be denied or abridged by the United States or by any State on account of sex

Congress shall have power to enforce this article by appropriate legislation.

Amendment XX

Section 1.

The terms of the President and the Vice President shall end at noon on the 20th day of January, and the terms of Senators and Representatives at noon on the 3d day of January, of the years in which such terms would have ended if this article had not been ratified; and the terms of their successors shall then begin.

Section 2.

The Congress shall assemble at least once in every year, and such meeting shall begin at noon on the 3d day of January, unless they shall by law appoint a different day.

Section 3.

If, at the time fixed for the beginning of the term of the President, the President elect shall have died, the Vice President elect shall become President. If a President shall not have been chosen before the time fixed for the beginning of his term, or if the President elect shall have failed to qualify, then the Vice President elect shall act as President until a President shall have qualified; and the Congress may by law provide for the case wherein neither a President elect nor a Vice President shall have qualified, declaring who shall then act as President, or the manner in which one who is to act shall be selected, and such person shall act accordingly until a President or Vice President shall have qualified.

Section 4.

The Congress may by law provide for the case of the death of any of the persons from whom the House of Representatives may choose a President whenever the right of choice shall have devolved upon them, and for the case of the death of any of the persons from whom the Senate may choose a Vice President whenever the right of choice shall have devolved upon them.

Section 5.

Sections 1 and 2 shall take effect on the 15th day of October

following the ratification of this article
.

Section 6.

This article shall be inoperative unless it shall have been ratified as an amendment to the Constitution by the legislatures of three-fourths of the several States within seven years from the date of its submission.

Amendment XXI

Section 1.

The eighteenth article of amendment to the Constitution of the United States is hereby repealed.

Section 2.

The transportation or importation into any State, Territory, or Possession of the United States for delivery or use therein of intoxicating liquors, in violation of the laws thereof, is hereby prohibited.

Section 3.

This article shall be inoperative unless it shall have been ratified as an amendment to the Constitution by conventions in the several States, as provided in the Constitution, within seven years from the date of the submission hereof to the States by the Congress.

Amendment XXII

Section 1.

No person shall be elected to the office of the President more than twice, and no person who has held the office of President, or acted as President, for more than two years of a term to which some other person was elected President shall be elected to the office of President more than once. But this Article shall not apply to any person holding the office of President when this Article was proposed by Congress, and shall not prevent any person who may be holding the office of President, or acting as President, during the term within which this Article becomes operative from holding the office of President or acting as President during the remainder of such term.

Section 2.

This article shall be inoperative unless it shall have been

ratified as an amendment to the Constitution by the legislatures of three-fourths of the several States within seven years from the date of its submission to the States by the Congress.

Amendment XXIII

Section 1.

The District constituting the seat of Government of the United States shall appoint in such manner as Congress may direct:

A number of electors of President and Vice President equal to the whole number of Senators and Representatives in Congress to which the District would be entitled if it were a State, but in no event more than the least populous State; they shall be in addition to those appointed by the States, but they shall be considered, for the purposes of the election of President and Vice President, to be electors appointed by a State; and they shall meet in the District and perform such duties as provided by the twelfth article of amendment.

Section 2.

The Congress shall have power to enforce this article by appropriate legislation.

Amendment XXIV

Section 1.

The right of citizens of the United States to vote in any primary or other election for President or Vice President, for electors for President or Vice President, or for Senator or Representative in Congress, shall not be denied or abridged by the United States or any State by reason of failure to pay poll tax or other tax.

Section 2.

The Congress shall have power to enforce this article by appropriate legislation.

Amendment XXV

Section 1.

In case of the removal of the President from office or of his death or resignation, the Vice President shall become President.

Section 2.

Whenever there is a vacancy in the office of the Vice President, the President shall nominate a Vice President who shall take office upon confirmation by a majority vote of both Houses of Congress.

Section 3.

Whenever the President transmits to the President pro tempore of the Senate and the Speaker of the House of Representatives his written declaration that he is unable to discharge the powers and duties of his office, and until he transmits to them a written declaration to the contrary, such powers and duties shall be discharged by the Vice President as Acting President.

Section 4.

Whenever the Vice President and a majority of either the principal officers of the executive departments or of such other body as Congress may by law provide, transmit to the President pro tempore of the Senate and the Speaker of the House of Representatives their written declaration that the President is unable to discharge the powers and duties of his office, the Vice President shall immediately assume the powers and duties of the office as Acting President.

Thereafter, when the President transmits to the President pro tempore of the Senate and the Speaker of the House of Representatives his written declaration that no inability exists, he shall resume the powers and duties of his office unless the Vice President and a majority of either the principal officers of the executive department or of such other body as Congress may by law provide, transmit within four days to the President pro tempore of the Senate and the Speaker of the House of Representatives their written declaration that the President is unable to discharge the powers and duties of his office. Thereupon Congress shall decide the issue, assembling within forty-eight hours for that purpose if not in session. If the Congress, within twenty-one days after receipt of the latter written declaration, or, if Congress is not in session, within twenty-one days after Congress is required to assemble, determines by two-thirds vote of both Houses that the President is unable to discharge the powers and duties of his office, the Vice President shall continue to discharge the same as Acting President; otherwise, the President shall resume the powers and duties of his office.

Amendment XXVI

Section 1.
 The right of citizens of the United States, who are eighteen years of age or older, to vote shall not be denied or abridged by the United States or by any State on account of age.

Section 2.
 The Congress shall have power to enforce this article by appropriate legislation.

Amendment XXVII

 No law, varying the compensation for the services of the Senators and Representatives, shall take effect, until an election of representatives shall have intervened.

A FEW NOTES ABOUT AMMENDMENTS

 For a proposed amendment to become law it must be submitted to the states for ratification. The Ratification process requires that 3/4s of the states approve the amendment. In 1789, that number of states was 9 of the 13 states, today that number is 38. There have been 33 proposed amendments submitted to the States for ratification, 27 of these have been ratified, 4 are still pending and 2 have failed the ratification process.

 The 4 pending proposals have been pending since 1789, 1810, 1861 and 1924 respectively and concern issues that are not relevant today. States normally have a 7 year period to ratify a proposal. After that period the proposal will expire as being deemed no longer pertaining to the nation. The 4 pending proposals where submitted before the time limit was placed and therefore can be pending literally forever. The 27th Amendment was submitted for ratification in 1789 and took 202 years to be ratified by 3/4 of the States and that number changed many times as new states were added to the Union.

BRANCHES OF GOVERNMENT

This is a brief description of the Branches of Government and their responsibilities as written into the Constitution.

There are 3 Branches of our Government: The Executive Branch, The Legislative Branch and The Judicial Branch.

The Executive Branch consists of the President and Vice President and the various executive Departments. i.e. Treasury, Defense etc., the Legislative Branch consists of the Senate and Congress and the Judicial Branch is the Supreme Court. Each of these Branches have specific duties assigned by the Constitution. I am not going into all of the duties, just the main function of each branch.

***

The Executive Branch: According to the Constitution, the Executive Branch must **"take care that the laws be faithfully executed", and "preserve, protect and defend the Constitution"**

***

The Legislative Branch (Congress): Congress consists of 2 parts, the Senate and the House of representatives. The Constitution grants numerous powers to Congress including;

House of Representatives - the powers to levy and collect taxes; to coin money and regulate its value; provide for punishment for counterfeiting, establish post offices and roads, issue patents, create federal courts inferior to the Supreme Court, combat piracies and felonies, declare war, raise and support armies, provide and maintain a navy, make rules for the regulation of land and naval forces, provide for, arm and discipline the militia, exercise exclusive legislation in the District of Columbia, and to make laws necessary to properly execute powers.

The Senate must approve many important Presidential appointments, including cabinet officers, federal judges (including nominees to the Supreme Court), department secretaries (heads of federal executive branch departments), U.S. military and naval officers, and ambassadors to foreign countries.

Any legislative proposal or bill must be passed by majority vote by both houses. The President may Veto the bill but it may still pass into law if passed by 2/3s vote from both houses.

***

The Judicial Branch: The U. S. Supreme Court adjudicates "cases and controversies" matters pertaining to the federal government, disputes between states, and interpretation of the United States Constitution, and, in general, can declare legislation or executive action made at any level of the government as unconstitutional, nullifying the law and creating precedent for future law and decisions. The United States Constitution does not grant the judicial branch the power of judicial review (the power to declare a law Unconstitutional). Judicial Review authority was added in 1803.

REFERENCES

Illustrations:
>   Statue of Liberty – Cover, Personal photos of
>   Dana Turk

Quotations:
>   Notable Quotes

References:
>   The U. S. Archives
>   The National Register
>   The Congressional Reports
>   Wikipedia
>   Flickr
>   The Creature from Jekyll Island by G. Edward
>   Griffn
>   Inside Congress by Ronald Kessler
>   Wall Street and the Rise of Hitler by Anthony
>   C. Sutton
>   Time Magazine
>   The Albuquerque Journal
>   KQRE News 13 Albuquerque New Mexico

VARIOUS READINGS

Ronald Kessler, Inside Congress, (1998) Pocket Books, New York, NY

Anthony C Sutton, Wall Street and the Rise of Hitler, (1976) "76 Press, Seal Beach, CA

G Edward Griffith, The Creature from Jekyll Island, A Second Look at the Federal Reserve, (1994), American Press, New York, NY

INTERNET REFERENCES

Wikipedia, www.wikipedia.com
Flickr, www.flickr.com
Snopes, www.snopes.com
Notable Quotes, www.notablequotes.com

www.ingramcontent.com/pod-product-compliance
Lightning Source LLC
Chambersburg PA
CBHW050448290526
45786CB00006B/2207